An Introduction to CATIA V6

Release 2012

(A Hands-On Tutorial Approach)

T0186866

Kirstie Plantenberg

University of Detroit Mercy

ISBN: 978-1-58503-663-9

SDC

PUBLICATIONS

Schroff Development Corporation

www.SDCpublications.com

Schroff Development Corporation
P.O. Box 1334
Mission KS 66222
(913) 262-2664
www.SDCpublications.com

Publisher: Stephen Schroff

PREFACE

An Introduction to CATIA (A Hands-On Tutorial Approach) is a collection of tutorials meant to familiarize the reader with CATIA's Mechanical Design and Shape workbenches. The reader is not required to have any previous CATIA knowledge. The workbenches covered in this book are; *Sketcher, Part Design, Assembly Design, Drafting, Generative Surface Design*, and *Imagine and Shape*. Preceding each tutorial is a brief description of the workbench, toolbars, and commands to be used and focused on within the tutorial. This book is not meant to be strictly a reference book. It is meant to enable the reader to get right into CATIA and start drawing. You will learn by doing. The author directs the reader to CATIA's online documentation for a more detailed description of the commands.

Suggested time line for a 15 week course

CATIA Tutorials	CATIA Exercises	Week
CATIA Basics: Tutorials 1.1, 1.2 & 2.1	Exercise 2.1	Week 1
Sketcher: Tutorials 2.2, 2.3, 2.4	Exercise 2.2, 2.3, 2.4	Week 2
Sketcher: Tutorials 2.5, 2.6, 2.7	Exercise 2.5, 2.6	Week 3
Part Design: Tutorials 3.1, 3.2, 3.3	Exercise 3.1, 3.2	Week 4
Part Design: Tutorials 3.4, 3.5	Exercise 3.3, 3.4	Week 5
Part Design: Tutorial 3.6, 3.7	Exercise 3.5	Week 6
Part Design: Tutorials 3.8, 3.9		Week 7
Assembly: Tutorials 4.1	Exercise 4.1 or 4.2	Week 8
Assembly: Tutorials 4.2		Week 9
Drafting: Tutorial 5.1 Generative Surface Design: Tutorials 6.1	Exercise 5.1	Week 10
Generative Surface Design: Tutorials 6.2, 6.3	Exercise 6.1	Week 11
Imagine and Shape: Tutorial 7.1, 7.2		Week 12
Imagine and Shape: Tutorial 7.3	Exercise 7.1	Week 13

NOTE: One week is left available for spring break or computer mishaps. Another week is left available for the final.

ACKNOWLEDGMENTS

I would like to thank my mother, Phyllis Plantenberg, for painstakingly going over and performing each tutorial. This was an invaluable service enabling me to correct mistakes, misinterpretations, and vagueness. I would also like to thank the University of Detroit Mercy for providing the tools necessary to make this book possible.

TABLE OF CONTENTS

Chapter 1: CATIA Basics

- Chapter 1 Introduction   1-1
- Tutorial 1.1: CATIA's interface and file management   1.1-1
- Tutorial 1.2: Selecting, Editing & Viewing Objects   1.2-1

Chapter 2: Sketcher

- Chapter 2 Introduction   2-1
- Tutorial 2.1: Sketch Work Modes   2.1-1
- Tutorial 2.2: Simple Profiles & Constraints   2.2-1
- Tutorial 2.3: Advanced Profiles & Sketch Analysis   2.3-1
- Tutorial 2.4: Modifying Geometries & Relimitations   2.4-1
- Tutorial 2.5: Axes & Transformations   2.5-1
- Tutorial 2.6: Operations on 3D Geometries & Sketch planes   2.6-1
- Tutorial 2.7: Points & Splines   2.7-1
- Exercises   2.8-1

Chapter 3: Part Design

- Chapter 3 Introduction   3-1
- Tutorial 3.1: Sketch-Based Features: Pads   3.1-1
- Tutorial 3.2: Sketch-Based Features: Pockets, Holes & Slots   3.2-1
- Tutorial 3.3: Sketch-Based Features: Shafts & Grooves   3.3-1
- Tutorial 3.4: Sketch-Based Features: Advanced commands   3.4-1
- Tutorial 3.5: Dress-Up Features: Drafts, Fillets & Chamfers   3.5-1
- Tutorial 3.6: Dress-Up Features: Shell, Thickness & Threads   3.6-1
- Tutorial 3.7: Transformation Features   3.7-1
- Tutorial 3.8: Boolean Operations   3.8-1
- Tutorial 3.9: Material Properties   3.9-1
- Exercises   3.10-1

Chapter 4: Assembly Design Fundamentals

- Chapter 4 Introduction   4-1
- Tutorial 4.1: Assembly Constraints and Advanced Commands   4.1-1
- Tutorial 4.2: Advanced Assembly   4.2-1
- Exercises   4.3-1

Chapter 5: Drafting Fundamentals

- Chapter 5 Introduction   5-1
- Tutorial 5.1: Generative Drafting   5.1-1
- Exercises   5.2-1

Chapter 6: Generative Surface Design Fundamentals

- Chapter 6 Introduction   6-1
- Tutorial 6.1: Wireframe toolbar   6.1-1
- Tutorial 6.2: Surfaces toolbar   6.2-1
- Tutorial 6.3: Operations toolbar   6.3-1
- Exercises   6.4-1

Chapter 7: Imagine and Shape Basics

- Chapter 7 Introduction   7-1
- Tutorial 7.1: Car Body   7.1-1
- Tutorial 7.2: Turbine Blade   7.2-1
- Tutorial 7.3: Tea Pot   7.3-1
- Exercises   7.4-1

Chapter 1: CATIA BASICS

INTRODUCTION

Chapter 1 focuses on CATIA's interface and file management. The tutorials within this chapter are meant to help the reader navigate through CATIA's workbenches as well as to show how objects are selected.

TUTORIALS CONTAINED IN CHAPTER 1

- Tutorial 1.1: CATIA's interface and file management
- Tutorial 1.2: Selecting, Editing & Viewing Objects

NOTES:

Chapter 1: CATIA BASICS

Tutorial 1.1:
CATIA's Interface and file management

FEATURED TOPICS & COMMANDS

COLLABORATING IN CATIA 2
   Life Cycle Operations 2
   Maturity States...2
   User Roles..3
STARTING CATIA...4
CATIA'S INTERFACE 5
VLM NAVIGATOR 6
MECHANICAL DESIGN WORKBENCHES 7
SHAPE WORKBENCHES 8
DOCUMENTS 8
TUTORIAL 1.1 START 9
   Section 1: CATIA's Workbenches 9
   Section 2: The Specification Tree...11
   Section 3: File Management..16
   Section 4: Using the Robot...17
   Section 5: Exporting and Importing 18

PREREQUISITE KNOWLEDGE & COMMANDS

* The windows operating system

COLLABORATING IN CATIA

CATIA provides tools for collaborative development of a product (i.e. bicycle, car or coffee maker). Using these tools enables you to interact with others on the design team during the design process. The design team can share data and work concurrently on the same design. CATIA enables you to do this by saving all files on a common database so that people with the correct permissions may access and edit any part in the product. It also gives the users the ability to send text messages, annotate parts, share snapshots and perform an online review.

In order to accomplish all of the above without chaos, the users designate where the product/part is the design cycle and assigns each member of the design team a role with inherent permissions.

Life Cycle Operations

The *Lifecycle* operations toolbar allows you to assign your product/part a position in the design cycle. Its position in the cycle determines whether or not the product/part can be modified, only viewed and who owns it. This becomes particularly important since all parts and products are saved in a common database. The commands in the *Lifecycle* toolbar reading left to right are;

- Lock: This command locks data to other users using the same database.
- Unlock: This commands unlocks data to other users using the same database.
- Version: This command allows you to create a new version of an object.
- Change status: This command allows you to change the maturity state of an object.
- Transfer ownership: This command allows you to transfer ownership of your object.
- Delete object: This command allows you to delete part references and part representations from the database.

Maturity States

A project/part may be assigned one of five maturity states as follows;

- In Work: An "in work" project/part implies that new versions are coming, the data is fully modifiable and it may be deleted.
- Released: "Released" projects/parts are ready for production or delivery. "Released" data is no longer modifiable and cannot be deleted.
- Frozen: A "frozen" project/part is an intermediate state between "in work" and "released". If can be used for projects/parts waiting to be approved or to keep an intermediate state of the design.
- Obsolete: "Obsolete" data are projects/parts that are no longer manufactured. "Obsolete" data may not be promoted or deleted.
- Removed: "Removed" data are in a recycle bin and are waited to either be reactivated or deleted.

User Roles

A person's role defines what they can access and modify. The different roles are;

- <u>ProjectAdministrator:</u> The administrator assigns roles to people.
- <u>ProjectLeader:</u> A project leader can edit and propagate (save) projects/parts, delete "in work" or "removed" data, export or import 3DXML data and release "frozen" data.
- <u>Creator:</u> A creator may edit, delete, freeze and propagate projects/parts that he/she owns. But may not do the same for a project/part that he/she does not own.
- <u>Experimenter:</u> An experimenter may edit projects/parts but may not propagate.
- <u>Viewer:</u> A viewer may access any "released" or "obsolete" project/part of any project and access any "frozen" project/part. A viewer cannot edit or propagate projects/parts.

Below are several tables that summarize the permissions of various roles on various maturity states.

In work data	Project Administrator	Project Leader	Creator	Experimenter	Viewer	Any role on another project
Access	√	√	√			
Manage	√	√	√			
Delete	√	√	√			
Version	√	√	√			
Promote	√	√	√			

Released data	Project Administrator	Project Leader	Creator	Experimenter	Viewer	Any role on another project
Access	√	√	√	√	√	√
Manage						
Delete						
Version	√	√				
Promote	√					

Obsolete data	Project Administrator	Project Leader	Creator	Experimenter	Viewer	Any role on another project
Access	√	√	√	√	√	√
Manage						
Delete						
Version						
Promote						

Removed data	Project Administrator	Project Leader	Creator	Experimenter	Viewer	Any role on another project
Access	√	√	√			
Manage						
Delete	√	√	√			
Version						
Promote	√	√	√			

Frozen data	Project Administrator	Project Leader	Creator	Experimenter	Viewer	Any role on another project
Access	√	√	√	√		√
Manage	√					
Delete						
Version	√	√	√			
Promote	√	√	√			

STARTING CATIA

To start CATIA, right click on the CATIA V6R2012 icon and select *Open*. A *Connect* window will appear (it may take awhile). The *Connect* window allows you to select your database and enter your user name and password. To select your role, type your password and then select the *Options* button. An *Options for ENOVIA V6* window will appear. Clicking on the *Select* button opens up a *Security Context Select* window which allows you to select your role.

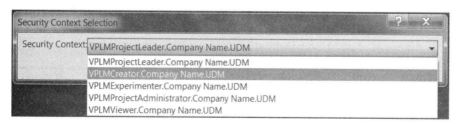

1.1 - 4

CATIA'S INTERFACE

CATIA's workbenches use icons and pull down menus to access commands. These two ways of accessing commands may be familiar to you. Many programs use these two methods. It is the environment inside the drawing area or document window that may take a while to get used to. Shown below are the main components of CATIA's user interface followed by a description of each area.

1. <u>Pull down menus:</u> All of the commands, options, and settings may be accessed in the pull down menus.
2. <u>Active workbench icon:</u> CATIA has several workbench environments. For example, the *Sketcher* workbench is used to sketch 2D profiles and the *Part Design* workbench is used to make solids from a sketch among other things. The active workbench icon shows the workbench you are currently working in.
3. <u>Workbench specific toolbars:</u> Each workbench has its own specific set of toolbars. However, some toolbars are common between workbenches.

4. Hidden toolbars: If there is not enough room to show all active toolbars, CATIA will hide some. You will know when some toolbars are hidden if a double arrow appears in one or more of the corners.

5. Status bar: The status bar tells the user what the program is expecting next. For example, if the *Circle* command is chosen, the prompt line will read *Select a point or click to define the circle center*. After the center point is selected it will read *Select a point or click to define the circle radius.*

6. Specification tree: The specification tree shows all the commands and sketches that were used to construct the part. The specification tree may be used to make changes to the part.

7. Robot: The robot is a graphic manipulator that lets you perform a certain number of manipulations on objects. The robot has three axes that represent the X, Y and Z axes. The sphere at the origin is the manipulation handle. The handle is used to drag the robot and place it on objects to be manipulated.

8. Coordinate planes: The default coordinate planes show the 3 mutually perpendicular Cartesian coordinate planes. 2D profiles may be sketched on these planes.

9. VLM navigator: Allows you to search and propagate data as well as to communicate with your design team.

10. Compass: The PLM compass is a permanent fixture in CATIA's interface that enables you to access detailed PLM information (people, shape, structure and links).

11. Active document window: CATIA allows multiple documents or parts to be open simultaneously. These documents can be arranged in the usual windows based placements such as Tiled horizontally and vertically, Cascaded, etc...

VLM NAVIGATOR

The VLM navigator bar shown has many functions that will be discussed below.

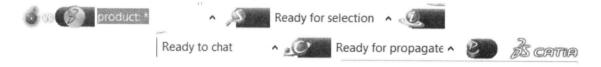

- Start: The start button allows you to start or switch between workbenches.

- Search: Semantic search enables you to search for products, parts, shapes, etc. Once a search has been performed, a *Name Like* window will appear with all the files that match the search criteria.

- Impact: Impact allows you to edit links contained in your product.

- Collaborate: Collaborate allows you to start an instant collaboration with a colleague.

- Propagate: (Ctrl + S) Clicking the propagate button propagates all the new and modified objects without displaying the propagate dialog box. Propagating a file saves it to the database.

MECHANICAL DESIGN WORKBENCHES

Listed below is a selected list of *Mechanical Design* workbenches along with a brief summary of their uses. The figure shows all of CATIA's Product lines and *Mechanical Design* workbenches.

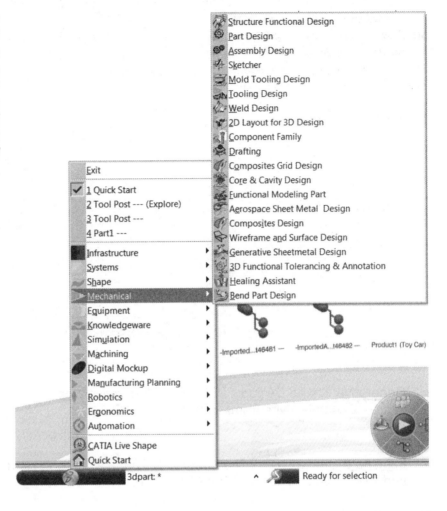

- **Part Design:** The *Part Design* workbench allows you to create a main solid from a sketch and then modify it by adding or removing material.

- **Sketcher:** The *Sketcher* workbench is used to create 2D profiles that may be used to create the initial solid, modify an existing solid, or used as a path or direction curve.

- **Assembly Design:** The *Assembly Design* workbench is used to assemble and constrain parts in an assembly.

- **Drafting:** The *Drafting* workbench is used to create 2D detailed and assembly drawings from 3D models.

SHAPE WORKBENCHES

Listed below is a selected list of *Shape* workbenches along with a brief summary of their uses. The figure shows all of CATIA's Product lines and *Shape* workbenches.

- Generative Shape Design: The *Generative Shape Design* workbench is used to create complex wire frame profiles and surfaces.

- Imagine & Shape: The *Imagine & Shape* workbench is used to create complex surfaces through a pull and stretch method.

DOCUMENTS

When working on a part or assembly in CATIA you are working within a document. The type of document depends on the workbench you are using to create and modify the geometry. When searching for a particular document, you must specify which type it is.

- Assembly (Product)
- Part Design, Sketcher, Generative Surface Design, Imagine and Shape (3DPart)
- Drafting (Drawing)

Shown on the next page, are 3 document windows open simultaneously in CATIA. There is an assembly of the product called *Machine Vise*, a part (the *Base*) belonging to the product and a 2D drawing of the *Base*.

TUTORIAL 1.1 START

The part modeled in this tutorial is simple and is used to familiarize you with CATIA's interface.

Section 1: CATIA's Workbenches

1) Launch CATIA by right clicking on the **CATIA V6R2012** icon and selecting **Open**.

(**IMPORTANT!** Be patient. This program takes a long time to load. Do not open the program twice.)

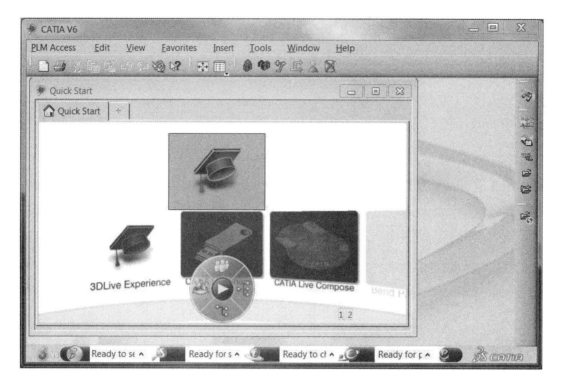

2) At the bottom, select **Start** 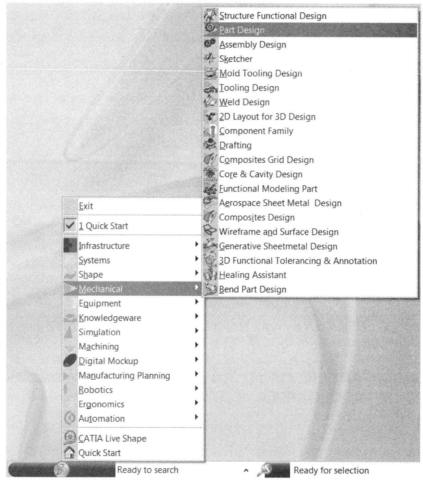 **– Mechanical – Part Design**.

3) A *3D Part / Physical Product* window will appear. Name your part **Plate** (in both the *3D Part* and *Physical Representation* tabs) and then select **Finish.** Maximize the *Plate* window if it is not already maximized. Notice the specification tree in the upper left corner. At the moment you have three coordinate planes and an empty *PartBody* and *Geometrical Set.*

Section 2: The Specification Tree

2.1 – Specification Tree Basics

In the upper left corner of the *Part/Plate* window, there is a specification tree. This contains all the planes, sketches, operations, and constraints, used to create the part. The specification tree can be expanded and collapsed by clicking on the '+' and '-' symbols (not present at the moment). The most important feature of the specification tree is that it allows you to view and modify the individual components and operations used to create the part. The specification tree is arranged in a hierarchical manner. At the top of the tree is the Part, under the Part there are 3 coordinate planes and an empty PartBody. The tree's structure depends on the type of document you are creating.

1) In the specification tree, click on the **xy plane**. Notice that the xy coordinate plane itself as well as its representation in the specification tree highlight. Repeat for each coordinate plane.

CATIA's interface allows you to reposition toolbars to suit your needs. Therefore, they may not always be located in their original position. By restoring the toolbars default position, locating specific icons throughout each tutorial is made easier.

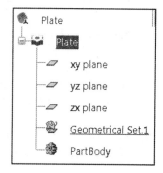

2) Restore the toolbars to their default positions. At the top pull down menu, select **Tools – Customize...**

3) In the *Customize* window, select the **Toolbars** tab and then select the **Restore all contents ...** button. In the *Restore All Toolbars* window, select **OK**. Select the **Restore position** button. In the *Restore All Toolbars* window select **OK** and then select **Close** in the *Customize* window.

This procedure should be repeated any time you are unable to locate a specific toolbar.

4) Make your *PartBody* the "In Work Object". Right click on the **PartBody** and select **Define In Work Object**. Notice that now the PartBody is underlined.

5) Enter the *Sketcher* Workbench on the xy plane. Select the **xy plane** in the specification tree or the coordinate plane itself. Then select the

   Sketcher icon . This is usually located in the right side toolbar area. In the *Sketcher* workbench a grid will appear and the environment will rotate such that you are viewing the xy plane.

6) Restore the toolbars default position as was done previously and drag the *User Selection Filter* and *Sketch Tools* toolbars to the top toolbar area.

7) Locate the *Profile* toolbar in the right side toolbar area. Click on the bar at the top of this toolbar and drag it to the center of the screen. (If the *Profile* toolbar is not there, right click on the right side toolbar area and activate the *Profile* toolbar. A toolbar is active if there is a check mark next to it.)

Click on the black arrow to reveal hidden icons.

Click on the bar to move toolbar.

8) If not already active, display your *Status Bar*. Select **View** - **Toolbars** - **Status Bar**. The *Status Bar* name should have a check next to it.

9) Click on the black arrow under the *Rectangle* icon to reveal the *Predefined Profile* toolbar.

Predefined Profile

10) Draw a Rectangle similar to the one shown. Use the grid as a guide. Select the **Rectangle** icon. It is located in the *Profile* toolbar. Notice that when you select the rectangle icon it turns orange. Down at the bottom of the screen the *Status Bar* will read *Select or pick first point to create the rectangle*. Once you select the first point, the prompt line will read *Select or pick second point to create the rectangle*. The *Status Bar* should be consulted whenever you are unsure what action to take next.

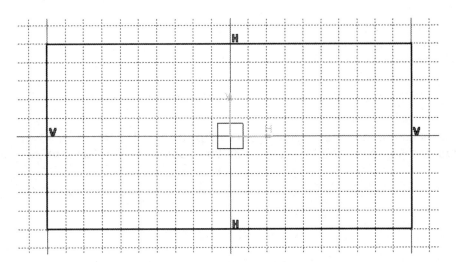

11) Exit the sketcher by selecting the **Exit workbench** icon .

12) Hit the **Esc** key twice or click on the graphics screen to deselect the rectangle. The rectangle should no longer be highlighted.

13) Click on the '+' symbol next to the *PartBody* to reveal *Sketch.1*.

14) Pad the rectangle to a length of 20 mm. Select the **Pad** icon . In the *Pad Definition* window, fill in the following fields;
   - Type: **Dimension**
   - Length: *20 mm*
   - The Selection: field should read No selection. Activate the Selection: field by clicking on No selection and then click on the rectangle. The Selection: field should now read **Sketch.1**. Select **OK**.

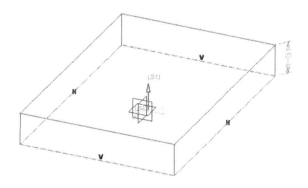

(**Problem?** If your units are in inches, select **Tools - Options....** In the *Options* window, select *Parameters and Measure* and then the *Units* tab. Select *Millimeter (mm)* as your Length units.)

15) Create a 20 mm hole in the top of the block. Click on the **Hole** icon located in the right side toolbar area. Notice that nothing happens. Read the *Status Bar*. Select the top face of the block near the middle. In the *Hole Definition* window and **Extension** tab, fill in the following fields;
- Select **Up To Last** in the top pull down field,
- Diameter: *20 mm*.

16) Expand your specification tree as shown. Notice that the *PartBody* in the specification tree is no longer empty. It contains a main solid (Pad.1) and a hole (Hole.1). Notice that each operation is based on a separate sketch.

2.2 – Manipulating the Specification Tree

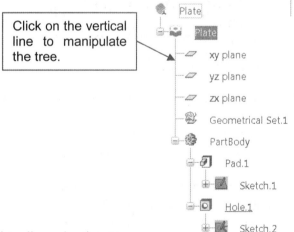

The specification tree may be moved, zoomed or hidden.

1) Click on one of the vertical connecting lines in the tree. Your part should turn faded. This indicates that the tree is active.

2) Move the tree down by clicking on the vertical line again and dragging it.

3) Zoom in on your tree by clicking and holding your middle mouse button, clicking your right mouse button once, and moving your mouse up and down.

4) Move the tree back to its original location in the upper left corner and zoom it to its normal size.

5) Click on the vertical connecting line again to deactivate the tree.

6) Hit the **F3** key on your keyboard to hide the tree and then hit it again to show the tree.

Section 3: File Management

1) Click on the **Propagate** button in the *VLM Navigator*. This will save your part to the database.

(**Problem ?** If you are unable to propagate your part, you may have entered CATIA under the wrong role. You need to be either a *Project Leader* or a *Creator* to propagate.)

2) Close the part. Select **PLM Access - Close**.

3) In the *Search* field (located in the VLM Navigator) type **3dpart: plate*** and then select the **Search** button   . A *Name Like plate** window will appear. This window will display all the parts and associated properties that match the search criteria.

#	Disp... name	Name	Ve...on	Identifier	Ve...nt	De...on	Creation date	Cr...om	Last modification	Maturity	Lo...ner	Resp...sible	Project
1	Plate ---	Plate	---	S3dp000522			7/15/2011 :: 4:33:00 PM		7/25/2011 :: 2:24:00 PM	REMOVED		udm24	UDM
2	Plate ---	Plate	---	S3dp000787			7/25/2011 :: 2:16:00 PM		7/25/2011 :: 2:16:00 PM	IN_WORK		udm24	UDM

4) Double click on **Plate**.

5) Open the part by selecting **PLM Access - Open - Open**.

6) Enter the *Sketcher* on the top face of the block. Select the **Sketcher** icon   and then select the top face of the block.

7) Draw a **Rectangle** in the approximate location and of approximate size as shown.

8) Exit the sketcher by selecting the **Exit workbench** icon .

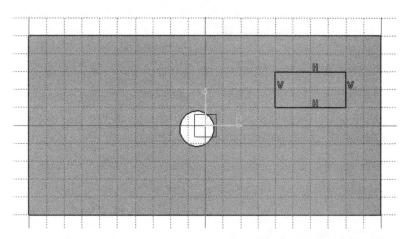

9) **Pad** the rectangle to a length of **40 mm**.

10) **Propagate** your part.

Section 4: Using the Robot

The *Robot* is used to translate and rotate the 3D environment and all of its components or an individual part.

1) Click and hold one of the straight lines of the robot and move your mouse. Notice that both the part and the coordinate planes translate.

2) Click and hold one of the curved lines of the robot and move your mouse. Notice that the part and the coordinate planes both rotate.

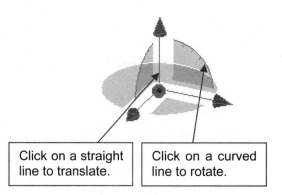

Click on a straight line to translate.

Click on a curved line to rotate.

3) Attach the robot to your part. Click and drag the origin of the robot and move it to the top of your part and release. The robot is attached to the part if the part becomes highlighted. If the robot did not attach, snap it back to its original position and try to attach it again.

4) **Propagate**.

Section 5: Exporting and Importing

In order to have a local file that can be placed on a memory device, the document must be *Exported*. The export type is 3DXML. This type of file can then be *Imported* into CATIA V6 and later releases of CATIA V5.

1) Export the document to a 3DXML file. The document may only be exported to 3dxml from the *Name Like *.** window. Select **Window - Name Like T11Plate**. Select the **T11Plate** document and then select **PLM Access - Export...** In the *Export* window select the ***.3dxml** format, choose a location for the file and name your file.

2) Import the newly created 3dxml file. Select **PLM Access - Import - 3D XML...** In the *Import 3D XML* window, select the location where you saved the file. CATIA should automatically detect all 3dxml file in this location. Select **T11Plate.3dxml** and then select **OK**.

3) After the file has been access and you can see a preview of the part, you need to open it. **Select PLM Access - Open - Open**.

NOTES:

NOTES:

Chapter 1: CATIA BASICS

Tutorial 1.2:
Selecting, Editing & Viewing Objects

FEATURED TOPICS & COMMANDS

SELECTING OBJECTS..2
    Simple Selection..2
    The Selection Toolbar 2
THE VIEW TOOLBAR 3
THE GRAPHIC PROPERTIES TOOLBAR..4
TUTORIAL 1.2 START 5
    Section 1: Selecting profiles and features 5
    Section 2: Undo/Redo 8
    Section 3: Scanning the design process 12
    Section 4: Viewing your part...12
    Section 5: Graphic Properties..13

PREREQUISITE KNOWLEDGE & COMMANDS

* Entering workbenches

SELECTING OBJECTS

Simple Selection

The left mouse button is used to select an object. You can select an object or feature on the physical part or you can click on the corresponding feature in the specification tree. To select multiple items hold the *control key* down while selecting. The selected item(s) will be highlighted in both the tree and the part.

The Selection Toolbar

There are several ways to select a feature. You can simply select the feature using your left mouse button or you can use one of the available traps. The *Selection* toolbar has 7 different trap options and is located near the top of the right side toolbar area. Reading the toolbar from left to right the commands are;

- Select: This allows you to select features by using your left mouse button. To multiple select you need to hold the control key down. This option is always active.
- Selection trap above Geometry: This option allows you to start the trap on a specific element and not on an empty space as with the other trap options.

- Rectangle Selection Trap: The selection trap allows you to create a window and select all features that are completely enclosed in that window.
- Intersecting Rectangle Selection Trap: The intersecting trap uses a window to select all items that are enclosed in or touching the window boundaries.
- Polygon Selection Trap: The polygon trap is similar to the selection trap but it enables you to create a window that is irregular.
- Free Hand Selection Trap: This selection trap allows you to create a free hand line. Everything that crosses this line is selected.
- Outside Trap Rectangle Selection: The outside trap selection selects everything that is outside the window.
- Intersecting Outside Rectangle Trap Selection: The intersecting outside trap selection selects everything that is outside and intersecting the window.

THE VIEW TOOLBAR

The *View* toolbar contains commands that allow you to manipulate (pan, rotate, zoom) your part and contains different viewing options. Reading the toolbar from left to right the options are;

- Fit All In: This zooms your part out or in to fit the available window space.
- Pan: Allows you to move your part around the screen without zooming.
- Rotate: Allows you to rotate your part to view different sides.
- Zoom In: Makes your part look bigger.
- Zoom Out: Makes your part look smaller.
- Normal View: It rotates the part to show you a 2D view of the object relative to a selected face.
- Create Multi-view: This command allows you to create four different independently controlled views of the part and/or sketch.
- Quick view toolbar: Allows you to view the part from the following different perspectives.
  - Isometric view
  - Front view
  - Back view
  - Left view
  - Right view
  - Top view
  - Bottom view

- View mode toolbar: Enables you to view the part in the following different modes.
  - Shading (SHD)
  - Shading with Edges
  - Shading with Edges without Smooth Edges
  - Shading with Edges and Hidden Edges
  - Shading with Material
  - Wireframe (NHR)
  - Customize View Parameters

- Hide/Show: Allows you to hide and show different features of a part.
- Swap visible space: This command hides everything that is showing and shows everything that is hidden.

THE GRAPHIC PROPERTIES TOOLBAR

The *Graphic Properties* toolbar allows you to change the fill color, line thickness and type, and transparency of an object among other things. The options in the *Graphic Properties* toolbar from left the right are;

- Fill Color: Allows you to change the color of a part.
- Transparency: You can make a part transparent so that you can see parts or features behind it.
- Line Weight: You can change the line thickness of a sketch.
- Line Type: You can change the line type of a sketch.
- Point Symbol: There are several different choices for point style.
- Painter: This allows you to match the color of one feature to the color of another.
- Wizard: The Wizard command allows you to view the graphic properties of different features of your part.

TUTORIAL 1.2 START

The part modeled in this tutorial is shown on the right. It will be used to illustrate how to edit, manipulate, view and change the graphic properties of a part.

Section 1: Selecting profiles and features

1) Launch **CATIA V6** and start a new 3D Part (**PLM Access - New**). Name the *3D Part* and the *Physical Representation **T12Seat***.

(**Note:** If all students in the class are using the same database, precede the *part name* with *your name* to uniquely identify your part (e.g. **Kirstie_T12Seat**.)

2) If not already there, enter the *Part Design* workbench (**Start** - **Mechanical - Part Design**)

3) Make your *PartBody* the "In Work" object. Right click on the *PartBody* and select **Define In Work Object**.

4) Enter the *Sketcher* workbench on the xy plane. Select the **xy plane** in the specification tree or the coordinate plane it self then select the

   Sketcher icon .

5) Turn the snap to grid option on. Select the

   Snap to Point icon. If the icon is orange, the snap is on, if it is blue, the snap is off. The *Snap to Point* icon is located in the *Sketch Tools* toolbar. This toolbar should be located at the top toolbar area where it was moved. If this toolbar is not active or you can't locate it, go to **Tools** – **Customize...** – **Toolbar** tab – **Restore all Content** and **Restore Position**.

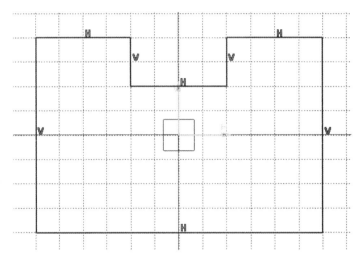

6) Select the **Profile** icon and draw the sketch shown. The profile command allows you to draw several continuous lines connected together. Count the grid spacing to determine the sketch size. Make sure the sketch is oriented around the origin as shown in the figure.

7) Click on the screen somewhere away from the sketch to deselect the profile. Nothing should be highlighted.

8) Left click on the left vertical line of the profile. Notice it highlights. Click on the bottom line in the profile. Notice that the bottom line highlights, but the vertical line is no longer highlighted. Hold the *control* key and click on the right side vertical line of the profile. Notice that the bottom line remains selected.

9) Deselect all. Click off of the profile or hit the **Esc** key twice.

10) Bring the **Select toolbar** out from underneath the **Select** icon and move it so that it stands alone.

11) In the *Select* toolbar, select the **Rectangle Selection Trap** icon. Draw the selection window shown by clicking and holding the mouse button and moving to the opposite corner. Notice that the only lines that where entirely enclosed in the window are selected.

12) Deselect all.

13) In the *Select* toolbar, select the **Intersecting Rectangle Selection Trap** icon. Draw a selection window like the previous window. Notice that this time all items that where enclosed in and touching the window are selected.

14) Deselect all.

15) In the *Select* toolbar, select the **Polygon Selection Trap** icon. Draw the selection window shown clicking the mouse at positions 1 to 4 in order. Double click at point 4 to end the window selection.

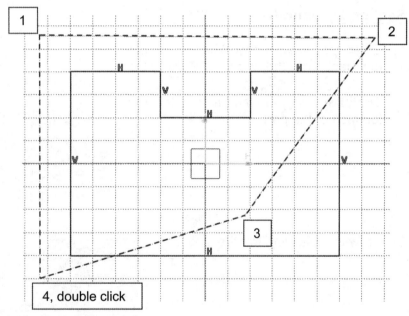

16) Deselect all.

17) Try the other trap commands and determine what they do.

18) Use the **Rectangle Selection Trap** to select the entire sketch.

19) Hold the **control** key and deselect the bottom line by clicking on it.

20) Close the **Select toolbar**.

21) Exit the sketcher by selecting the **Exit workbench** icon.

22) Pad the profile to a length of 20 mm. Select the **Pad**

     icon. In the *Pad Definition* window fill in the following fields;
- **Type: Dimension**
- **Length: *20 mm***
- **Selection: Sketch.1**

Section 2: Undo/Redo

1) Enter the *Sketcher* workbench on the top face of the part. Select the

   Sketcher icon and then select the top face of the part.

   Sketch face

2) Draw the following **Profile**.

3) **Exit** the Sketcher and **Pad** the sketch to a length of **50 mm**.

4) **Propagate** your part.

5) Enter the **Sketcher** on the **zx plane**.

6) Draw the **Line** shown in white.

7) **Exit** the Sketcher.

8) Select the **Stiffener** icon. This is located in the *Sketch Based Features* toolbar. It may be stacked under the **Solid Combine** icon. Create a stiffener using **Sketch.3** that is *1 mm* thick and is **From the Side**.

Sketch face

9) Enter the **Sketcher** on the front face of the part.

10) Draw 2 **Rectangles** as shown.

11) **Exit** the Sketcher.

12) Create pockets using the two rectangles. The *Pocket* command removes material. Select the **Pocket** icon and use the **Up to Last** option (this means through all).

13) **Propagate** your part.

14) Expand your specification tree to the sketch level as shown.

15) Select **Stiffener.1** in the specification tree. Notice that this feature is highlighted in the specification tree as well as in the part.

16) Right click on **Stiffener.1** and select **Delete**. Select **OK** in the *Delete* window.

17) At the top pull down menu, select **Edit** – **Undo**. Alternatively, you can select the **Undo** icon, or use the keyboard shortcut **CTRL + Z**.

18) Right click on **Sketch.3** (the sketch associated with the stiffener) and select **Hide/Show**. Now we can see the sketch used to create the stiffener.

19) Select the **Undo/Redo Overview** icon. Your undo history should look similar to the one shown. There may be some extra steps depending on what you have done. Select **(Pocket)**. This will select all commands performed before the *Pocket* as well as the *Pocket* command. Select the **Undo** icon within the window and then **Close**.

20) Select the **Redo** icon or use the keyboard shortcut **CTRL + Y** to get the *Pocket* back.

Section 3: Scanning the design process

This allows you to view the part's history step by step in order to see the design process.

1) At the top pull down menu, select **Edit – Scan or Define In Work Object...**

2) In the *Scan* window, select the **First** button, then scroll through the design process using the **Next** button. When complete, select the **Exit** button.

Section 4: Viewing your part

The part can be manipulated (Pan, Rotate, Zoom) using the icons in the *View* toolbar or by using the mouse buttons. Given below is a description of how to use a three button mouse to manipulate your part.

- Pan = Hold the middle mouse button and move the mouse.
- Zoom = Hold the middle mouse button, click and release the right mouse button and move the mouse.
- Rotate = Hold the middle mouse button, click and hold the right or left mouse button and move the mouse.

1) Use the icons in the *View* toolbar to **Pan**, **Rotate**, and **Zoom** your part. This toolbar is located in the bottom toolbar area. It may be hidden in the bottom right corner.

2) Use your mouse buttons to Pan, Rotate and Zoom your part.

3) Select the **Fit All In** 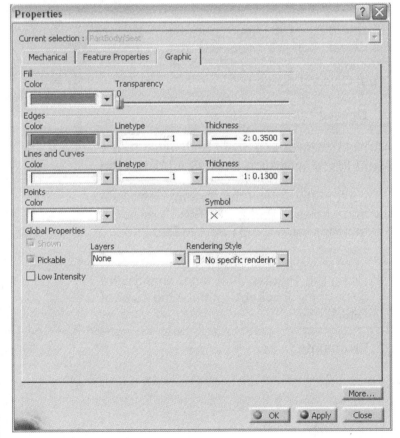 icon.

4) View your object from the **Top view** , then the **Right view** , and then the **Isometric view** .

5) Select different view modes and notice the differences . Go back to **Shaded with Edges** when finished.

Section 5: Graphic Properties

Parts in CATIA can be assigned different colors. This is very helpful especially when viewing an assembly.

1) In your specification tree, right click on **PartBody** and select **Properties**.

2) In the *Properties* window, select the *Graphic* tab. Under the Fill Color field select the color **red** and select **Apply**. Notice that the entire part changes to red. Then, under the Edges Color field select the color **green** and select **OK**.

3) Deselect all.

4) In your specification tree, right click on **Stiffener.1** and select **Properties**. Set the fill color to **tan**.

5) At the top pull down menu, select **View – Toolbars – Graphic Properties**. The *Graphics Properties* toolbar should appear.

6) In the specification tree, select **Pad.2** and change its fill color to **cyan** (light blue) using the *Graphic Properties* toolbar.

Fill color   Transparency

7) In the specification tree, select **Stiffener.1** and change its Transparency to **50%** using the *Graphic Properties* toolbar.

8) Using the **control** key, pick both surfaces that were used to sketch the pocket shapes as shown in the figure and change their color to **cyan** (light blue).

(**Problem?** Did your pockets disappear. If so, you did not complete the *Scan or Define in Work Object* process.)

9) Deselect all.

Select these surfaces.

10) Hold **control key** down and select **Pad.1** in the specification tree. Still holding the control key, select the **Painter** icon and select **Pad.2**. This procedure matches the color of Pad.1 to Pad.2.

11) Using the **Painter** icon, change the color of the **Pocket.1** to make the color of **Pad.1**.

12) **Propagate**

Chapter 2: SKETCHER

INTRODUCTION

Chapter 2 focuses on CATIA's *Sketcher* workbench. The reader will learn how to sketch and constrain very simple to very complex 2D profiles.

TUTORIALS CONTAINED IN CHAPTER 2

- Tutorial 2.1: Sketch Work Modes
- Tutorial 2.2: Simple Profiles & Constraints
- Tutorial 2.3: Advanced Profiles & Sketch Analysis
- Tutorial 2.4: Modifying Geometries & Relimitations
- Tutorial 2.5: Axes & Transformations
- Tutorial 2.6: Operations on 3D Geometries & Sketch planes
- Tutorial 2.7: Points & Splines

NOTES:

**Chapter 2:
SKETCHER**

*Tutorial 2.1: Sketch Work
Modes*

FEATURED TOPICS & COMMANDS

THE SKETCHER WORKBENCH 2

Sketcher workbench specific toolbars 2

THE SKETCH TOOLS TOOLBAR 3

TUTORIAL 2.1 START 4

Section 1: Using Snap to Point... 4

Section 2: Using construction elements..7

Section 3: Geometrical and Dimensional Constraints 9

Section 4: Cutting the part by the sketch plane. 12

PREREQUISITE KNOWLEDGE & COMMANDS

- Entering workbenches
- Entering and exiting the *Sketcher* workbench
- Drawing simple profiles
- Simple Pads and Pockets

THE SKETCHER WORKBENCH

The *Sketcher* workbench contains a set of tools that help you create and constrain 2D geometries. Solid features such as pads, pockets and shafts are created or modified using these 2D profiles. You can access the *Sketcher* workbench in various ways. Two simple ways are by using the top pull down menu (Start – Mechanical – Sketcher), or by selecting the *Sketcher* icon. When you enter the *Sketcher*, CATIA requires that you choose a plane to sketch on. You can choose this plane either before or after you select the *Sketcher* icon. To exit the sketcher, select the *Exit Workbench* icon.

Sketcher workbench specific toolbars

The *Sketcher* workbench contains the following standard workbench specific toolbars.

- Profile toolbar: The commands located in this toolbar allow you to create simple geometries (rectangle, circle, line, etc...) and more complex geometries (profile, spline, etc...).

- Operation toolbar: Once a profile has been created, it can be modified using commands such as trim, mirror, chamfer, and other commands located in the *Operation* toolbar.

- Constraint toolbar: Profiles may be constrained with dimensional (distances, angles, etc...) or geometrical (tangent, parallel, etc...) constraints using the commands located in the *Constraint* toolbar.

- Sketch tools toolbar: The commands in this toolbar allow you to work in different modes which make sketching easier.

- User Selection Filter toolbar: Allows you to activate different selection filters.

- Visualization toolbar: Allows you to, among other things to cut the part by the sketch plane and choose lighting effects and other factors that influence how the part is visualized.

- Tools toolbar: Allows you to, among other things, to analyze a sketch for problems, and create a datum.

THE SKETCH TOOLS TOOLBAR

The *Sketch tools* toolbar contains icons that activate and deactivate different work modes. These work modes assist you in drawing 2D profiles. Reading from left to right, the toolbar contains the following work modes; (Each work mode is active if the icon is orange and inactive if it is blue.)

- Grid: This command turns the sketcher grid on and off.
- Snap to Point: If active, your cursor will snap to the intersections of the grid lines.
- Construction / Standard Elements: You can draw two different types of elements in CATIA a *standard* element and a *construction* element. A standard element (solid line type) will be created when the icon is inactive (blue). Standard elements are used to create a feature in the *Part Design* workbench. A construction element (dashed line type) will be created when the icon is active (orange). Construction elements are used to help construct your sketch, but will not be used to create features.
- Geometric Constraints: When active, geometric constraints will automatically be applied such as tangencies, coincidences, parallelisms, etc...
- Dimensional Constraints: When active, dimensional constraints will automatically be applied when corners (fillets) or chamfers are created, or when quantities are entered in the value field. The value field is a place where dimensions such as line length and angle are manually entered.

TUTORIAL 2.1 START

The part modeled in this tutorial is shown below. The part is constructed with the assistance of different work modes.

Section 1: Using Snap to Point

1) Open a **New 3D Part** and name the part and its representation *T21Spline*.

2) Make your **PartBody** the **In Work Object**.

3) Enter the **Sketcher** on the **yz plane**.

4) Restore the default positions of the toolbars (**Tools – Customize... – Toolbars** tab – **Restore all contents... & Restore position**.) Move the *Sketch Tools* toolbar and the *User Selection Filter* toolbar to the top toolbar area.

5) Set your grid spacing to 100 mm. At the top pull down menu, select **Tools – Options...** In the *Options* window, expand the **Mechanical** portions of the left side navigation tree and select **Sketcher**. In the Grid section, activate the following checkboxes and fill in the following fields:

- Activate Display, Snap to point, and Allow Distortions.
- Set your Primary spacing and Graduations to H: *100 mm* and *20*, and V: *100 mm* and *10*.

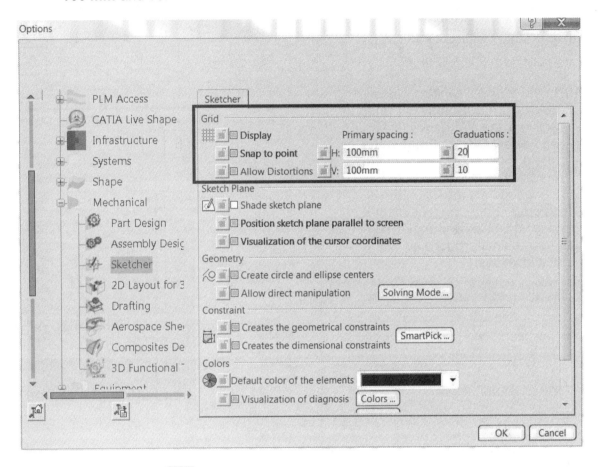

6) Select the **Spline** icon located in the *Profile* toolbar in the right side toolbar area. This is <u>not</u> the *Curve Filter* icon located in the *User Selection Filter* toolbar

7) In your *Sketch Tools* toolbar, activate your **Grid** icon and your **Snap to Point** icon. They should be orange (active). Move your cursor around the screen.

Note that it snaps to the intersections of the grid. Deactivate the **Snap to Point** icon by clicking on it and turning it back to blue. Move your cursor around the screen and notice the difference.

8) Reactivate the **Snap to Point** icon and draw the spline shown. Select each point (indicated by a number in a square) in order from 1 to 7, double clicking at the last point to end the spline command.

9) Edit the spline by double clicking on any portion of it.

10) In the *Spline Definition* window, select **CtrlPoint.7**, then activate the **Tangency** option, and select **OK**. Notice that the last point is now tangent to the first point.

(**Problem?** If the tangency is not working, go back and make sure that your points are located in the correct locations.)

11) Draw a **Circle** inside the spline as shown.

12) **Exit** the Sketcher and **Pad** the sketch to a length of *50 mm*.

13) **Propagate**.

Section 2: Using construction elements.

1) Deselect all.

2) Enter the **Sketcher** on the front face of the part.

3) Deselect all. Hit the **Esc** key twice.

4) Activate the **Construction/Standard Elements** icon. It should be orange.

5) Project an outline of the part onto the sketch plane. Select the **Project 3D Elements** icon then select the face of the part. This icon is located in the *Operations* toolbar near the bottom of the right side toolbar area. It may be hidden in the bottom right corner. Notice that a dashed sketch has appeared on the outline of the spline shape and the hole.

6) Deselect all. The projection should now be yellow (this means it is associated with the part and will change with the part) and dashed (this means it is a construction element).

Sketch face

7) Deactivate your **Grid** , **Snap to Point** , and **Construction / Standard Elements** icons.

8) Activate your **Geometrical constraints** and **Dimensional constraints** icons. They should be orange.

9) Using the **Profile** command to draw a triangle that looks like the one shown. The points of the triangle should lie on the projected construction element. You will know when you are on the projection when a symbol of two concentric circles appears, and you will know when you are snapped to the endpoint of the start point when a symbol of two concentric circles appears and the inner one is filled.

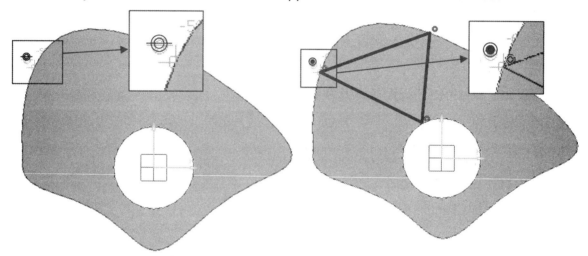

10) **Exit** the Sketcher and **Pad** the sketch to a length of **10 mm**.

Section 3: Geometrical and Dimensional Constraints

1) Deselect all.

2) Enter the **Sketcher** on the front large face of the part.

3) Your **Geometrical Constraints** icon should be active. It should be orange.

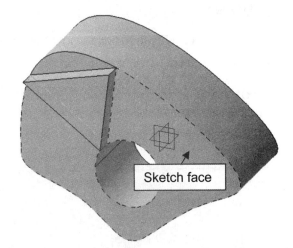

Sketch face

4) At the top pull down window, select **T**ools – **Options** – **Sketcher**. Under the Constraint portions of the window, select

SmartPick... The *SmartPick* window shows all the geometrical constraints that will be created automatically. These constraints may be turn on and off depending on your design/sketch needs. **Close** both the *Smart Pick* and *Options* windows.

5) Draw a **Rectangle** to the right of the hole as shown. Notice that geometric constraints (H = horizontal, V = Vertical) are automatically applied.

6) Deactivate the **Geometrical Constraints** icon and draw a **Rectangle** to the left of the hole as shown. Notice that no geometric constraints are made.

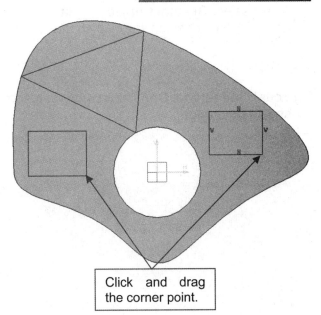

Click and drag the corner point.

7) For each rectangle, click on one of the points defining a corner and move it using the mouse (see figure on the previous page). Notice the difference between the two. This is due to the horizontal and vertical constraints that were applied to the one rectangle.

8) Undo (**CTRL + Z**) the moves until the original rectangles are back.

9) **Exit** the Sketcher and **Pocket** the sketch using the **Up to last** option.

10) Expand the specification tree to the sketch level.

11) **Propagate**.

12) Edit Sketch.3 (the sketch associated with the pocket). In the specification tree, double click on **Sketch.3**, or right click on it and select **Sketch.3 object - Edit**. You will automatically enter the sketcher on the sketch plane used to create this sketch.

13) Your **Dimensional Constraint** icon should be active. It should be orange.

14) Select the **Corner** 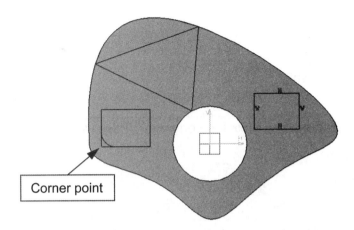 icon, select the bottom left corner point of the left rectangle, move your mouse up and to the right, and click. A corner or fillet will be created. The corner icon is located in the *Operations* toolbar near the bottom of the right side toolbar area. The corner/fillet may also be created by selecting the two lines that create the corner. Notice that a dimension is automatically created.

Corner point

15) Deactivate the **Dimensional Constraint** icon. It should be blue. Create a

Corner in the upper right corner of the same rectangle. Notice that this time no dimensional constraint was created.

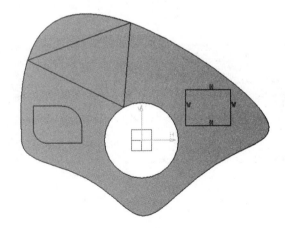

16) Reactivate the **Dimensional Constraint** icon and **Geometrical Constraint** icon. They should be orange.

17) **Exit** the Sketcher . We have changed the sketch used to create the pocket. Notice that the pocket is automatically updated to reflect these changes.

18) **Propagate**.

Section 4: Cutting the part by the sketch plane.

Sometimes it is necessary to sketch inside the part. The *Cut Part by Sketch Plane* command allows you to see inside the part and makes it easier to draw and constrain your sketch.

1) Deselect all.

2) Enter the **Sketcher** on the **xy plane**.

3) Select the **Isometric View** icon. This icon is located in the bottom toolbar area.

4) Select the **Cut Part by Sketch Plane** icon located in the bottom toolbar area. The part in now cut by the xy plane (the sketch plane).

5) Select the **Top view** icon and draw a **Circle** in the middle of the hole as shown in the figure.

6) **Exit** the Sketcher.

7) Select the **Pad** icon and then select the **More>>** button. Fill in the following fields for both the First and Second Limits;

- Type: **Up to surface**
- Limit: Select the inner circumference of the hole (for both limits)
- Selection: **Sketch.4** (the circle).

Select **Preview** to see if the Pad will be applied correctly, and then **OK**.

8) **Propagate**.

NOTES:

NOTES:

Chapter 2: SKETCHER

Tutorial 2.2: Simple Profiles & Constraints

FEATURED TOPICS & COMMANDS

PROFILE TOOLBAR 2

    Profile toolbar 2

    Predefined Profile toolbar 3

    Circle toolbar 3

    Spline toolbar 4

    Conic toolbar 4

    Line toolbar 4

    Point toolbar 4

CONSTRAINT TOOLBAR 5

SELECTING ICONS 5

TUTORIAL 2.2 START 6

    Section 1: Creating circles. 6

    Section 2: Creating dimensional constraints. 8

    Section 3: Creating lines. 9

    Section 4:   Creating geometrical constraints. 13

    Section 5: Creating arcs 16

    Section 6: Adding Text 19

PREREQUISITE KNOWLEDGE & COMMANDS

- Entering workbenches
- Entering and exiting the *Sketcher* workbench
- Simple Pads
- Work modes (Sketch tools toolbar)

PROFILE TOOLBAR

The *Profile* toolbar contains 2D geometry commands. These geometries range from the very simple (point, rectangle, etc...) to the very complex (splines, conics, etc...). The *Profile* toolbar contains many sub-toolbars. Most of these sub-toolbars contain different options for creating the same geometry. For example, you can create a simple line, a line defined by two tangent points, or a line that is perpendicular to a surface.

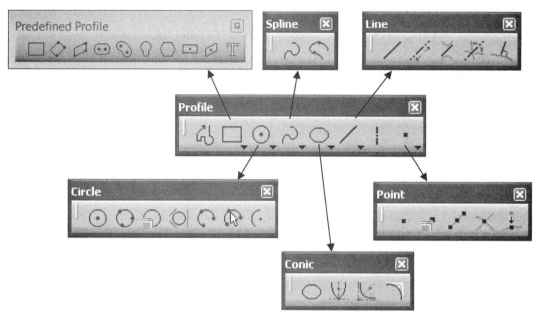

Profile toolbar

Reading from left to right, the *Profile* toolbar contain the following commands.

- **Profile:** This command allows you to create a continuous set of lines and arcs connected together.
- **Rectangle / *Predefined Profile* toolbar:** The default top command is *rectangle*. Stacked underneath are several different commands used to create predefined geometries.
- **Circle / *Circle* toolbar:** The default top command is *circle*. Stacked underneath are several different options for creating circles and arcs.
- **Spline / *Spline* toolbar:** The default top command is *spline* which is a curved line created by connecting a series of points.
- **Ellipse / *Conic* toolbar:** The default top command is *ellipse*. Stacked underneath are commands to create different conic shapes such as a hyperbola.
- **Line / *Line* toolbar:** The default top command is *line*. Stacked underneath are several different options for creating lines.
- **Axis:** An axis is used in conjunction with commands like mirror and shaft (revolve). It defines symmetry. It is a construction element so it does not become a physical part of your feature.
- **Point / *Point* toolbar:** The default top command is *point*. Stacked underneath are several different options for creating points.

Predefined Profile toolbar

Predefined profiles are frequently used geometries. CATIA makes these profiles available for easy creation which speeds up drawing time. Reading from left to right, the *Predefined Profile* toolbar contains the following commands.

- Rectangle: The *rectangle* is defined by two corner points. The sides of the rectangle are always horizontal and vertical.
- Oriented Rectangle: The *oriented rectangle* is defined by three corner points. This allows you to create a rectangle whose sides are at an angle to the horizontal.
- Parallelogram: The *parallelogram* is defined by three corner points.
- Elongated Hole: The elongated hole or slot is defined by two points and a radius.
- Cylindrical Elongated Hole: The *cylindrical elongated hole* is defined by a cylindrical radius, two points and a radius.
- Keyhole Profile: The *keyhole profile* is defined by two center points and two radii.
- Hexagon: The *hexagon* is defined by a center point and the radius of an inscribed circle.
- Centered Rectangle: The *centered rectangle* is defined by a center point and a corner point.
- Centered Parallelogram: The *centered parallelogram* is defined by a center point (defined by two intersecting lines) and a corner point.
- Text: Creates text that may be used to create a solid.

Circle toolbar

The *Circle* toolbar contains several different ways of creating circles and arcs. Reading from left to right, the *Circle* toolbar contains the following commands.

- Circle: A *circle* is defined by a center point and a radius.
- Three Point Circle: The *three point circle* command allows you to create a circle using three circumferential points.
- Circle Using Coordinates: The *circle using coordinates* command allows you to create a circle by entering the coordinates for the center point and radius in a *Circle Definition* window.
- Tri-Tangent Circle: The *tri-tangent circle* command allows you to create a circle whose circumference is tangent to three chosen lines.
- Three Point Arc: The *three point arc* command allows you to create an arc defined by three circumferential points.
- Three Point Arc Starting With Limits: The *three point arc starting with limits* allows you to create an arc using a start, end, and midpoint.
- Arc: The *arc* command allows you to create an arc defined by a center point, and a circumferential start and end point.

Spline toolbar

Reading from left to right, the *Spline* toolbar contains the following commands.

- Spline: A spline is a curved profile defined by three or more points. The tangency and curvature radius at each point may be specified.
- Connect: The connect command connects two points or profiles with a spline.

Conic toolbar

Reading from left to right, the *Conic* toolbar contains the following commands.

- Ellipse: The ellipse is defined by a center point and major and minor axis points.
- Parabola by Focus: The parabola is defined by a focus, apex and start and end points.
- Hyperbola by Focus: The hyperbola is defined by a focus, center point, apex and start and end points.
- Conic: There are several different methods that can be used to create conic curves. These methods give you a lot of flexibility when creating the above three types of curves.

Line toolbar

The *Line* toolbar contains several different ways of creating lines. Reading from left to right, the *Line* toolbar contains the following commands.

- Line: A line is defined by two points.
- Infinite Line: Creates infinite lines that are horizontal, vertical or defined by two points.
- Bi-Tangent Line: Creates a line whose endpoints are tangent to two other elements.
- Bisecting Line: Creates an infinite line that bisects the angle created by two other lines.
- Line Normal to Curve: This command allows you to create a line that starts anywhere and ends normal or perpendicular to another element.

Point toolbar

The *Point* toolbar contains several different ways of creating points. Reading from left to right, the *Point* toolbar contains the following commands.

- Point by Clicking: Creates a point by clicking the left mouse button.
- Point by using Coordinates: Creates a point at a specified coordinate point.

- <u>Equidistant Points:</u> Creates equidistant points along a predefined path curve.
- <u>Intersection Point:</u> Creates a point at the intersection of two different elements.
- <u>Projection Point:</u> Projects a point of one element onto another.

CONSTRAINT TOOLBAR

Constraints can either be dimensional or geometrical. Dimensional constraints are used to constrain the length of an element, the radius or diameter of an arc or circle, and the distance or angle between elements.

Geometrical constraints are used to constrain the orientation of one element relative to another. For example, two elements may be constrained to be perpendicular to each other. Other common geometrical constraints include parallel, tangent, coincident, concentric, etc... Reading from left to right:

- <u>Constraints Defined in Dialoged Box:</u> Creates geometrical and dimensional constraints between two elements.
- <u>Constraint:</u> Creates dimensional constraints.
  - o <u>Contact Constraint:</u> Creates a contact constraint between two elements.
- <u>Fix Together:</u> The fix together command groups individual entities together.
  - o <u>Auto Constraint:</u> Automatically creates dimensional constraints.
- <u>Animate Constraint:</u> Animates a dimensional constraint between to limits.
- <u>Edit Multi-Constraint:</u> This command allows you to edit all your sketch constraints in a single window.

SELECTING ICONS

When an icon is selected, it turns orange indicating that it is active. If the icon is activated with a single mouse click, the icon will turn back to blue (deactivated) when the operation is complete. If the icon is activated with a double mouse click, it will remain active until another command is chosen or if the Esc key is hit twice.

TUTORIAL 2.2 START

The part modeled in this tutorial is shown on the right. This part will be created using simple profiles, circles, arcs, lines, and hexagons. The geometries are constrained to conform to certain dimensional (lengths) and geometrical constraints (tangent, perpendicular, etc...).

Section 1: Creating circles.

(Hint: If you get confused about how to apply the different commands that are used in this tutorial, read the *Status Bar* for additional help.)

1) Open a **New 3D Part** and name your part and its representation **T22Post**.

2) Make your **PartBody** the **In Work Object**.

3) Enter the **Sketcher** on the **zx plane**.

4) Turn your **Grid** on.

5) Set your grid spacing to be **100 mm** with **10** graduations, activate the *Snap to point*, and activate the *geometrical* and *dimensional* constraints. (**Tools – Options...**)

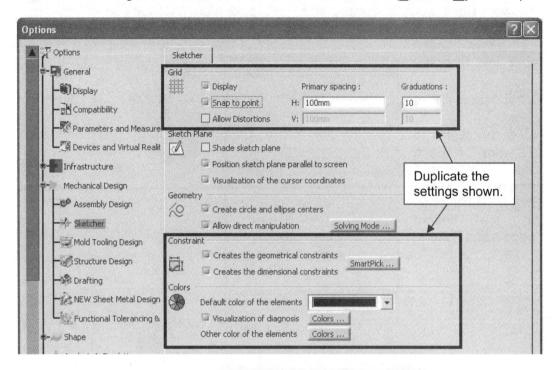

6) Pull out the **Circle** subtoolbar .

7) Double click on the **Circle** icon and draw the circles shown. Don't worry about the size, just make sure that the circle centers are in line with the **V** axis.

8) **Exit** the Sketcher and **Pad** the sketch to **12 mm** on each side (**Mirrored extent**). Notice that the inner circle at the bottom becomes a hole.

Section 2: Creating dimensional constraints.

1) Expand your specification tree to the sketch level.

2) Edit Sketch.1. To edit a sketch you can double click on the sketch name in the specification tree, or you can *right click* on the name select **Sketch.1 - Edit**. CATIA automatically takes you into the sketcher on the plane used to create Sketch.1.

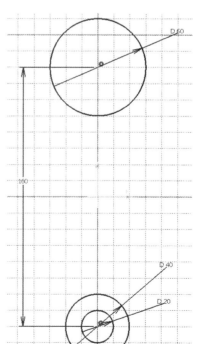

3) Double click on the **Constraints** icon.

4) Select the border of the upper circle, pull the dimension out and click your left mouse button to place the dimension. Repeat for the two bottom circles.

5) Select the center point of the upper circle, then the center point of the lower circles, pull the dimension out and click.

6) Double click on the dimensions to edit their sizes. In the *Constraint Definition* window, change the dimensions to what you see in the figure.

7) **Exit** the Sketcher and deselect all. Notice that the part automatically updates to the new sketch dimensions.

Section 3: Creating lines.

1) Deselect all.

2) Enter the **Sketcher** on the **zx plane**.

3) Deactivate the **Snap to Point** and the **Construction/Standard Elements** icons.

4) Project the two outer circles of the part onto the sketch plane as Standard elements.

   Double click on the **Project 3D Elements** icon. This icon is located in the *Operation* toolbar in the right side toolbar area. Select the outer edges of the two cylinders. If done correctly, the circumference of each circle will be outlined by a yellow circle.

5) Pull out the *line* toolbar .

6) Pull out the **Relimitations** toolbar located in the *Operation* toolbar.

7) Double click on the **Bi-Tangent Line** icon. Draw two tangent lines by selecting the points, in order, as indicated on the figure.

8) Double click on the **Quick trim** icon. Select the outer portion of the projected circles. Notice that the trimmed projection turns into a construction element (dashed).

9) **Exit** the Sketcher and **Pad** the sketch to *6 mm* on each side (**Mirrored extent**).

10) **Propagate**

11) Enter the **Sketcher** on the **zx plane**.

12) Activate the **Construction/Standard Element** icon (it should be orange).

13) Select the **Project 3D Elements** icon and then project the left line of the part as shown in the figure. The projected line should be dashed.

14) Activate your **Snap to Point** icon.

15) Draw a **Line** from point 1 to the origin and another **Line** from point 1 to point 2.

16) Draw a line that bisects the previous 2 lines using the **Bisecting Line** icon. Read the prompt line for directions.

17) Deactivate your **Snap to Point** icon.

18) Deselect all.

19) Deactivate the **Construction/Standard Element** icon (it should be blue now).

Projected line

Bisecting line

1

2

20) Draw a circle that is tangent to the projected line, normal line and bisecting line using the **Tri-Tangent Circle** 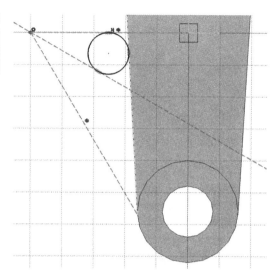 icon. Read the prompt line for directions.

21) Zoom in on the circle.

22) Using **Profile** , draw the three additional lines shown in the figure. When creating the line that touches the circle, both the construction line and the circle should turn orange before the point is selected.

23) Use the **Quick Trim** command to trim off the inside portion of the circle as shown. You will have to apply the quick trim operation twice.

24) Draw a **Hexagon** that has the same center as the circle/arc and is the approximate size shown in the figure. The *Hexagon* icon is usually stacked under the *Rectangle* icon. (Your hexagon will contain many constraints that are not shown in the figure.)

25) Deselect all.

26) Apply a dimensional **Constraint** to the distance between the flats of the hexagon as shown. To create this constraint, select the top line and then the bottom line. Double click on the dimension and change its value to **7 mm**.

27) **Exit** the Sketcher and **Pad** the sketch to a length of **2 mm** on each side (**Mirrored extent**).

28) **Propagate**

Section 4: Creating geometrical constraints.

1) Enter the **Sketcher** on the flat face of the large cylinder.

Sketch face

2) Deactivate the **Geometrical Constraint** icon (it should be blue). This will allow you to create profiles with no automatically applied constraints.

3) On the face of the large cylinder, draw the **Profile** shown. No geometrical constraints should be indicated.

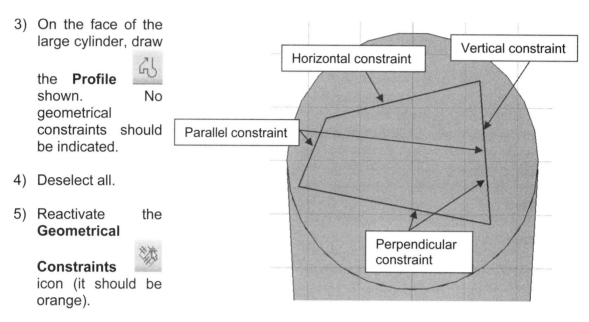

4) Deselect all.

5) Reactivate the **Geometrical Constraints** icon (it should be orange).

6) Apply a vertical constraint to the right line of the profile by right clicking on it and selecting **Line.? object – Vertical**. Don't worry if your sketch moves off the face of the object.

7) Apply a horizontal constraint to the top line using a similar procedure.

8) Deselect all.

9) Apply a perpendicular constraint between the right and bottom line of the profile. Hold the CTRL key down and select the left and bottom lines. Select the **Constraints Defined in Dialog Box** icon. In the *Constraint Definition* window, check the box next to **Perpendicular** and then select **OK.**

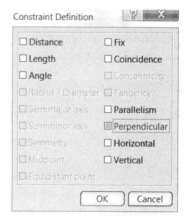

10) Apply a parallel constraint between the left and right lines of the profile in a similar way.

11) Drag the rectangle on to the surface of the part.

12) Apply **Constraints** to the rectangle and change their values to the values shown in the figure.

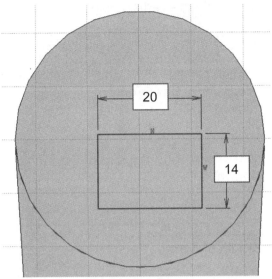

13) Apply the additional dimensional constraints shown in order to position the rectangle. Select the **Constraints** icon, then the circumference of the circle and then the appropriate side of the rectangle. Notice that once all the constraints are applied, the rectangle turns green indicating that it is fully constrained. If it did not turn green make sure the *Visualization of diagnosis* is activated in the *Options* window. (Tools – Options...)

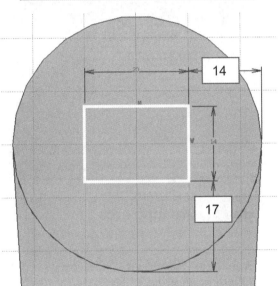

14) Draw the triangle shown using the **Profile** command. When drawing the triangle make sure that the top point is aligned with the origin (⊙) and the bottom line is horizontal (H).

15) Constrain the vertical height of the triangle to be **6 mm**. Select the **Constraints** icon, select one of the angled lines of the triangle, right click and select **Vertical Measure Direction** and place the dimension.

16) **Constrain** the rest of the triangle as shown.

17) **Exit** the Sketcher and **Pad** the sketch to a length of **5 mm.**

(**Problem?** If your sketch disappeared, *Copy* and *Paste* the sketch as described in the preface.)

18) **Propagate**.

Section 5: Creating arcs.

1) Enter the **Sketcher** on the front face of the middle section.

Sketch face

Face/Pad.2/PartBody

2) Activate the **Construction/Standard Element** icon.

3) Select the **Project 3D Elements** icon and then project the front face of the middle section.

4) Deselect all.

5) Deactivate the **Construction/Standard Element** icon.

6) Activate your **Snap to Point** icon.

7) Draw the profile shown. Use the **Three Point Arc** command to create the bottom arc, the **Arc** command to create the top arc. The *Arc* icons are stacked under the *Circle* icon. For assistance in creating the arcs, read the prompt line at the bottom of the graphics screen. Use the **Profile** command to create the connecting lines.

Arc

Center point for arc

Three point arc

8) **Exit** the Sketcher and

   Pad the sketch to a length of **30 mm.**

9) Deselect all.

10) Mirror the entire solid. Select the **Mirror** icon in the *Transformation Features* toolbar. Select the mirror element/face. In the *Mirror Definition* window select **OK**.

Mirroring element

Section 6: Adding Text.

1) Enter the **Sketcher** on the surface shown.

Sketch Face

2) Using the **Text** command (*Predefined Profile* toolbar), write your first name on the part. You may have to adjust the size of the text depending on how long or short your name is.

3) **Exit** the Sketcher and **Pocket** the sketch to a length of *10 mm*.

4) **Propagate**

Chapter 2: SKETCHER

Tutorial 2.3: Advanced Profiles & Sketch Analysis

FEATURED TOPICS & COMMANDS

OPEN AND CLOSED PROFILES 2

THE VALUE FIELD 3

SKETCH STATUS 3

SKETCH ANALYSIS AND SKETCH SOLVING STATUS 4

TUTORIAL 2.3 START 5

    Section 1: Using the value field. 5

    Section 2: Sketch Analysis 8

    Section 3: Solving for the sketch status... 12

PREREQUISITE KNOWLEDGE & COMMANDS

- Entering workbenches
- Entering and exiting the *Sketcher* workbench
- Simple profiles
- Simple pads and pockets
- Applying dimensional and geometric constraints
- Work modes (*Sketch tools* toolbar)

OPEN AND CLOSED PROFILES

A profile is a series of geometric elements (points, lines, arcs, etc...) connected together. Profiles are used to create or modify solids. If they are not constructed properly, CATIA will not allow you to perform certain operations in the *Part Design* workbench. Most operations such as *Pad* and *Pocket*, with some exceptions, require that a profile be closed and not self intersecting.

- <u>Open profile:</u> A profile is open when the first and last elements of the series are not connected.

- <u>Closed profile:</u> A profile is closed when the last element connects up with the first element in the series.

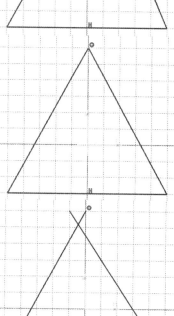

- <u>Self intersecting profile:</u> A self intersecting profile has at least two elements crossing each other.

- <u>Inner profiles:</u> Inner profiles are closed profiles inside other closed profiles. The operation performed on an inner profile is opposite to the operation performed on the outer profile. For example, if the outer profile is padded then the inner profile is pocketed.

THE VALUE FIELD

When sketching in the *Sketcher* workbench, a value field appears that allows you to enter exact coordinates, lengths, angles and radii. The value field attaches itself to the *Sketch tools* toolbar. For example, consider the value field when the *Profile* command is active. For the first point of the profile, you can enter a horizontal and vertical coordinate in the value field. The 'Tab' key is used to access the H: and V: value fields. The 'Enter' key should not be used when entering values in the value field.

If you are drawing a line, the second point of the profile can be defined by a coordinate point (H,V) or a length and an angle (L,A).

For an arc, the second point is defined by a coordinate point (H,V) and the radius (R) of the arc may also be entered.

Each 2D geometry (Line, Rectangle, Elongated Hole, Arc, etc...) has its own specific value field that allows you to control the geometric characteristics of that geometry.

SKETCH STATUS

The sketch status tells you if your sketch is under-constrained, over-constrained, or iso-constrained. Without constraints (geometrical and dimensional) a sketch can be moved freely just by clicking and dragging on an element. This could cause problems. If an element within the sketch is moved, it affects the solid that the sketch supports and any part that is related to the solid through assembly constraints. Therefore, it is important to completely constrain each sketch. If a sketch is completely constrained, it turns green.

- Under-constrained: A sketch is under-constrained when it is not completely constrained. In simple terms, there is not enough given information to duplicate the sketch exactly.
- Over-constrained: A sketch is over-constrained when there are duplicate dimensions given. The dimensions will turn purple when it is over-constrained. The duplicate dimension may be deleted or converted into a reference dimension.
- Iso-constrained: A sketch is iso-constrained when the sketch is completely constrained and there are enough dimensions and constraints given to duplicate the sketch exactly.

- <u>Inconsistent constraints:</u> Inconsistent constraints are constraints that conflict. For example, a parallel and perpendicular constraint applied to the same two lines is inconsistent or impossible. If there are inconsistent constraints present, the part will turn red.

SKETCH ANALYSIS AND SKETCH SOLVING STATUS

Within the *Tools* toolbar there is a *2D Analysis* subtoolbar containing commands that will help determine the sketch status and analyze sketch problems.

- <u>Sketch Solving Status icon:</u> This command will tell you if your sketch is under, over, or iso-constrained.

- <u>Sketch Analysis icon:</u> This command analyzes your sketch to determine problem areas. For example, it will identify any place where your sketch is open or intersecting, and it will identify duplicate and inconsistent constraints.

TUTORIAL 2.3 START

The part modeled in this tutorial is shown on the right. The main or outer profile is created using the help of the value field. The profiles used to modify the main pad are constructed in such a way as to illustrate the usefulness of solving for sketch status and analyzing sketches.

Section 1: Using the value field.

1) Start a **New 3D Part** and name your part and representation *T23Wedge*.

2) Make your **PartBody** the **In Work Object**.

3) Enter the **Sketcher** on the **yz plane**.

4) Enter your *Options* window (**Tools – Options...**). In the *Sketcher* section, activate the grid's *Display* and *Snap to Point* options, and set the snap spacing for both directions to be: Primary spacing = *100 mm,* Graduations = *10 mm.* In the *Constraint* section, activate both the *Dimensional* and *Geometrical constraints*.

5) Locate your *Sketch tools* toolbar and pull it out.

6) Select the **Profile** icon. Notice that a value field attaches itself to your *Sketch tools* toolbar.

7) Position your cursor at **-70,70** and click your left mouse button.

8) Type **140** in the L: field and hit the **TAB** key (do not hit the enter key).

9) Move your cursor around the screen. Notice that the angle of the line changes, but the length is constrained to be 140 mm and does not change.

10) Hit the **TAB** key until the A: field is activated, type **0**, and hit the **TAB** key. Notice that dimensions are automatically applied for every value that was typed in the value field.

(Having trouble? If your value field is not retaining the values that you type, move the cursor off the graphics screen and try again. If the cursor moves on the graphics screen, the values in the value field change to match the cursor position.)

11) Use the same procedure to make the next two lines. First line: L = **50** and A = **30**, Second line: L = **95** and A = **270**.

12) In the value field, click on the **Tangent arc** icon. Notice that the field options change.

13) Enter **60** in the R: field, and hit the **TAB** key.

14) Move your cursor around the graphics screen. Notice that the end point of the arc changes but not the radius.

15) Move your mouse until a vertical constraint line appears and click for the endpoint of the arc. The arc should travel through 90°.

16) Using the value field, create two more lines: H = *-70*, V = *-60*, and then H = *-70*, V = *-40*.

17) In the value field, click on the **Three point arc** icon. Type the following values for the arcs second point: H = *-50*, V = *-30*.

Three point arc

18) Move your mouse around the graphics screen and notice that the radius of the arc changes.

19) Type the following values for the arcs third point: H = *-40*, V = *-10*.

20) Create a **Line** (select this in the value field) whose endpoint is H = *-40*, V = *10*.

21) Create a **Three point arc** whose second point is H = *-30*, V = *20* and whose radius is R = *20*.

22) Move your mouse around the graphics screen. Notice that radius does not change. Move the mouse until the end point is directly above the start point of the arc and click.

23) Snap to profile's start point.

(Notice that every value that was entered into the value field has a dimension associated with it.)

24) **Exit** the *Sketcher* and **Pad** the sketch to a length of *50 mm*.

Section 2: Sketch Analysis

1) **Propagate**.

2) Enter the **Sketcher** on the left face of the part.

Sketch face

3) Draw the **Profile** shown in the figure. Double click at the last point to end the *Profile* command.

4) Select the **Sketch Analysis** icon. This is located in the *Tools* toolbar and usually found in the top toolbar area. The *Sketch Analysis* icon is usually stacked under the *Solve Sketch Status* icon.

5) A *Sketch Analysis* window will appear. Select the **Geometry** tab. In the Detailed information area, it should say that your profile is open. Notice that on your sketch two blue circles appear that identify the open section.

6) **Close** the *Sketch Analysis* window.

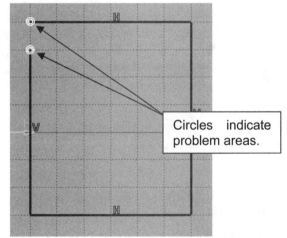

Circles indicate problem areas.

7) Draw a **Line** that starts at the end of the open vertical line and crosses the top horizontal line of the sketch.

8) **Exit** the *Sketcher* and try to apply a **Pocket** to the sketch. An error window will appear. This is because the profile is self intersecting. Select **OK** in the error window and **Cancel** the *Pocket Definition* window.

9) Edit **Sketch.2** (the most recent sketch). This may be done by double clicking on the sketch in the tree or on the part, or right clicking on Sketch.2 in the specification tree and selecting Sketch.2 object – Edit.

10) Select the **Sketch Analysis** icon.

11) A *Sketch Analysis* window will appear. Select the **Geometry** tab. In the *Detailed information* area, it should say that your profile is autocrossing or self intersecting. Notice that on your sketch two blue circles appear that identify the problem area.

12) **Close** the *Sketch Analysis* window.

13) Select the **H** constraint of the top horizontal line and hit the **Delete** key.

14) Drag the lines left endpoint up to coincide with the top endpoint of the angled line to create a closed profile.

15) Perform a **Sketch Analysis** and notice that the sketch is now closed.

16) Draw a **Circle** inside the profile as shown in the figure.

17) **Exit** the *Sketcher* and

Pocket to the sketch to a depth of **20 mm**. Notice that the outer profile is pocketed and the inner profile is not.

18) Enter the **Sketcher** on the left face of the part.

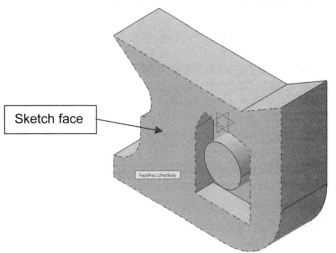

Sketch face

19) On your own, do your best to create the **Elongated Hole** shown. Remember to read the prompt line for help. The *Elongated Hole* icon is stacked under the *Rectangle* icon.

20) **Exit** the *Sketcher* and

Pocket to the sketch using the option of **Up to Last**.

Section 3: Solving for the sketch status.

1) Rotate the part so that you can see the back face of the part. You may do this by using the middle + right mouse buttons, or by using the compass.

2) Enter the **Sketcher** on the face indicated in the figure.

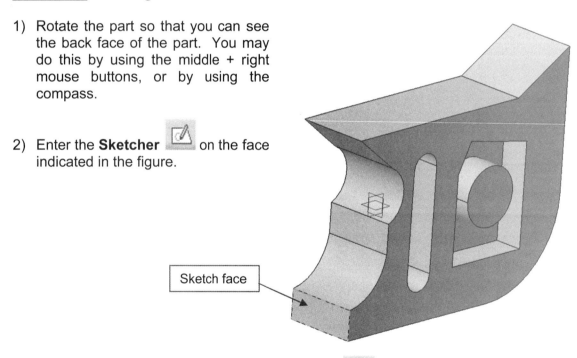

Sketch face

3) Activate your **Construction/Standard Element** icon.

4) Use the **3D Project Element** icon to project the edges indicated in the figure onto the sketch plane.

5) Deselect all.

6) Deactivate your **Construction/Standard Element** icon.

7) Draw the **Rectangle** shown making sure to make coincidence constraints with the top and bottom projected lines. You will know if a coincident constraint is applied if a double circle symbol appears. Notice that the top and bottom lines are green. They are constrained.

8) Select the **Sketch Solving Status** 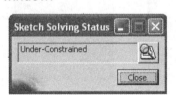 icon. A *Sketch Solving Status* window will appear and tell you that the sketch is under-constrained. **Close** the *Sketch Solving Status* window.

9) **Constrain** the rectangles width (*10 mm*) and distance from the side of the part (*20 mm*) as shown in the figure. Notice that once the constraints are applied, the rectangle turns green.

10) Select the **Sketch Solving Status** icon. A *Sketch Solving Status* window will appear and tell you that the sketch is iso-constrained (completely constrained). **Close** the *Sketch Solving Status* window.

Projected edges

11) **Constrain** 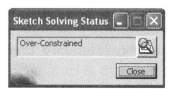 the rectangles height as shown in the figure. Notice that the dimension is purple indicating that it is a duplicate dimension.

12) Use the **Sketch Solving Status** icon to determine the sketch status.

13) Double click on the duplicate height dimension. In the *Constraint Definition* window activate the **Reference** toggle. Notice the parentheses now enclose the dimension value and the rectangle again becomes iso-constrained.

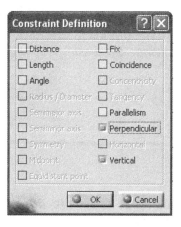

14) Apply a perpendicular constraint between the left and right vertical lines of the rectangle. Select the left and right vertical lines using the **CTRL** key. Select the **Constraint Definition** icon and activate the **Perpendicular** toggle. Notice that part of the rectangle turns pink or red indicating inconsistent constraints.

15) Use the **Sketch Solving Status** 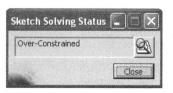 icon to determine the sketch status.

16) Select the perpendicular constraint line between the left and right sides of the rectangle and delete it. The rectangle should now be iso-constrained.

17) **Exit** the *Sketcher* and **Pad** the rectangle up to the curved surface. In the *Pad Definition* window;

- Type: **Up to Surface**,
- Limit: select the curved surface as shown in the figure.
- If you get an error window, select the **Reverse Direction** in the *Pad Definition* window.

18) **Propagate**

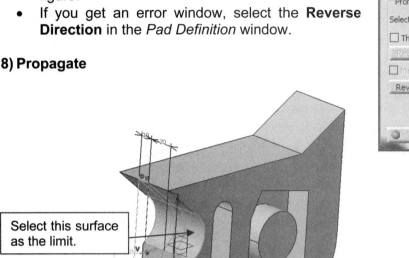

Select this surface as the limit.

NOTES:

Chapter 2: SKETCHER

Tutorial 2.4: Modifying Geometries & Relimitations

FEATURED TOPICS & COMMANDS

MODIFYING GEOMETRIES USING THE MOUSE 2

THE OPERATION TOOLBAR..2

THE RELIMITATIONS TOOLBAR 3

TUTORIAL 2.4 START 4

    Section 1: Modifying geometries with the mouse 4

    Section 2: Re-limiting geometries...6

    Section 3: Corners and Chamfers 8

PREREQUISITE KNOWLEDGE & COMMANDS

- Entering workbenches
- Entering and exiting the *Sketcher* workbench
- Work modes (*Sketch tools* toolbar)
- Creating profiles
- Applying dimensional and geometric constraints
- Editing a preexisting sketch
- Simple pads and pockets
- Rotating the part using the mouse or compass

MODIFYING GEOMETRIES USING THE MOUSE

The mouse can be used to move different elements of a sketch just by clicking and dragging that element. The way in which the element moves depends on the constraints that are present. For example, a horizontally constrained line can be moved anywhere but it will always remain horizontal.

THE OPERATION TOOLBAR

The *Operation* toolbar contains commands that allow you to modify and transform elements of a sketch. The commands contained in the *Operation* toolbar from left to right are

- Corner toolbar:
  - The *Corner* toolbar contains commands that create fillets. The *Corner* command creates a rounded corner. When selected, five options appear in the *Sketch tools* toolbar. Each option is a different method of dealing with the corner after the fillet is applied. The options from left to right are: *Trim all Elements, Trim First Element, No Trim, Standard Line Trim, Construction Line Trim,* and *Construction Lines No Trim.*
  - The *Tangent Arc* command creates a fillet that is tangent to only one surface.

- Chamfer: The *Chamfer* command creates an angled corner. When selected, five options appear in the *Sketch tools* toolbar. Each option is a different method of dealing with the corner after the chamfer is applied. The options from left to right are: *Trim all Elements, Trim First Element, No Trim, Standard Line Trim, Construction Line Trim* and *Construction Lines No Trim.*

- Relimitations toolbar: This toolbar contains commands that allow you to re-limit or modify 2D geometries. It contains commands such as *Trim, Break,* and *Close.*
- Transformation toolbar: This toolbar contains commands that allow you to duplicate and modify existing geometries. The commands from left to right are: *Mirror, Symmetry, Translate, Rotate, Scale,* and *Offset.*
- 3D Geometry toolbar: This toolbar contains commands that allow you to use 3D geometries to create 2D sketches. The commands from left to right are: *Project 3D Elements, Intersect 3D Elements, Project 3D Silhouette Edges* and *Project 3D Canonical Silhouette Edges.*

THE RELIMITATIONS TOOLBAR

The *Relimitations* toolbar contains commands that allow you to re-limit or modify 2D geometries. The commands from left to right are

- Trim: The *Trim* command allows you to delete unwanted portions of an element. The *Trim* command allows you to dynamically choose how you want the element trimmed. When selected, two options appear in the *Sketch tools* toolbar: *Trim All Elements* and *Trim First Element*. If you are unfamiliar with this command, it may be a bit confusing.
- Break: The *Break* command allows you to break one element into two.
- Quick Trim: The *Quick Trim* command allows you to delete unwanted portions of an element. When selected, three options appear in the *Sketch tools* toolbar: *Break and Rubber In, Break and Rubber Out*, and *Break and Keep*. When the *Break and Rubber In* option is selected, the selected element will be automatically trimmed between the two closest limiting elements. When the *Break and Rubber Out* option is selected, the selected element will be kept and the elements on the outside of the two closest limiting elements will be automatically trimmed. When the *Break and Keep* option is selected, the selected element will be broken at the two closest limiting elements.
- Close: The *Close* command creates a complete circle out of an arc. This command may also be used on ellipses.
- Complement: The *Complement* command erases an arc and creates its complement. This command may also be used on ellipses.

TUTORIAL 2.4 START

Two different views of the part modeled in this tutorial are shown on the right. The main focus of this tutorial is to modify and relimit geometries. While constructing the first sketch, the mouse will be used to move and modify the sketch. Modifications to the main pad will be constructed using the commands located in the *Operation* and *Relimitations* toolbars.

Section 1: Modifying geometries with the mouse.

1) Start a **New 3DPart** and name it *T24Angled*.

2) Make your **PartBody** the **In Work Object**.

3) Enter the **Sketcher** on the **xy plane**.

4) Activate **Geometrical** and **Dimensional** Constraints (orange), and deactivate the **Snap to Point** (blue).

5) Draw a **Rectangle** similar to that shown in the figure. Since the geometrical constraints are active, horizontal and vertical constraints are automatically applied.

6) Deselect all.

7) Using your mouse, click and drag the right side vertical line to the left. Notice that the horizontal and vertical constraints are maintained, but the rectangle may move up and down because it is not constrained in space.

8) Click and drag the bottom right corner point up and to the left.

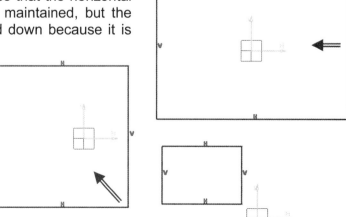

9) **Constrain** ⊟ the **left** and **top** lines of the rectangle as shown. (In this instance, only select one line when constraining. Do not select 2 lines to place one dimension.)

10) Click and drag the rectangle to the center. Notice that the whole rectangle moves. The rectangle is completely constrained with respect to itself, but it is not constrained in space and therefore is not green.

11) **Constrain** ⊟ the rectangle in space as shown. Notice that the rectangle is now iso-constrained and is green.

12) Try to move the rectangle with the mouse. You should not be able to.

13) **Exit** ⬆ the *Sketcher*

and **Pad** ⬛ the sketch to a length of **100 mm**.

14) Edit Sketch.1.

15) Delete the 50 mm constraint that fixes the rectangle to V axis.

16) Delete the bottom horizontal (H) and right side vertical (V) constraints, and the constraints (dimensions) locating the rectangle in space.

17) Click and drag the bottom right corner point up and to the left.

18) **Exit** the *Sketcher*. Notice that the Pad.1 is automatically updated to reflect the changes made in the sketch.

Section 2: Re-limiting geometries

1) Deselect all.

2) Enter the **Sketcher** 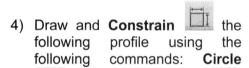 on the right face of the part.

Sketch face

3) Pull out the *Relimitations* toolbar.

4) Draw and **Constrain** the following profile using the following commands: **Circle** , **Bi-Tangent Line** . When completed, your sketch should be iso-constrained. You may not need to place the 50 mm constraint if you made your circles coincident with the V axis. (Note: The 50 mm dimension may not be necessary if you constrained the centers to the V axis.)

D30

D30

Trimmed elements

50

25

45

50

5) Trim the part of the circles that lie between the tangent lines. Double click on the **Quick Trim** icon and then select the parts of the circles that lie between the tangent lines as indicated in the figure. Hit the **ESC** key to exit the *Quick Trim* command.

(Note: If we tried to pad the sketch as is, CATIA would give us an error of self intersecting elements. Therefore, we need to break the tangent lines where they cross.)

6) Select the **Break** icon and then select the lines one after the other. Read the prompt line to understand why you are selecting the lines. Select the **Break** icon again. This time select the lines in reverse order.

7) **Exit** the *Sketcher* and **Pad** the sketch to a length of *40 mm*.

8) Deselect all.

9) Enter the **Sketcher** on the face of one of the padded circles as indicated in the figure.

Sketch face

10) Use the **3D Project Elements** icon to project both arcs onto the sketch plane. Note that they are yellow and still associated with the part.

(Note: We are going to use the *Close* and *Complement* commands on these projected arcs. These commands cannot be performed on associated (yellow) elements. Therefore, we need to disassociated or isolate the elements from the part.)

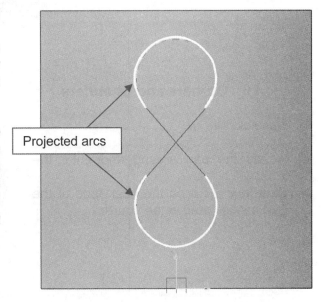

Projected arcs

11) Isolate the projected elements. Use the **CTRL** key and mouse to select both projected elements. At the top pull down menu, select **Insert – Operation – 3D Geometry – Isolate**. Notice that the elements are no longer yellow.

12) On your own, use the **Close** command to close the top arc and the **Complement** command to create a complement of the bottom arc. Then, draw a **Line** between the endpoints of the bottom arc.

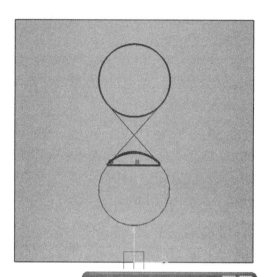

13) **Exit** the *Sketcher* and **Pad** the sketch to a length of *10 mm*.

14) **Propagate**.

Section 3: Corners and Chamfers

1) Deselect all.

2) Rotate the part around and enter the **Sketcher** on the back face of the part as indicated in the figure.

Sketch face

3) Draw and **Constrain** the two

Rectangles shown in the figure. Place the constraints on the sides shown. (Constrain the length of the rectangle sides by selecting two lines instead of one.)

4) Use **Quick Trim** to trim off the inside lines of the rectangle as shown.

5) Apply *Corners* (fillets) to the inside corners of the sketch and change the dimension values to those shown in the figure. The corners should be applied with the *trim all* option activated. For the **8 mm**

corner, select **Corner** and then select the corner point. Pull the radius out and click. Change the dimension value by double clicking on the dimension. For the **5**

mm corner, select **Corner** and then select both lines that make the corner.

6) Apply a **Chamfer** to the upper right corner of the sketch of length **10 mm** and angle **45°**.

(Problems?
- If an error window appears telling you the it is impossible to trim a lengthed element, select **Yes**.
- If an error window appears telling you that you are about to apply inconsistent constraints, get out of the Chamfer command and do the following. Delete the 25 mm and 20 mm height and width dimensions of the upper rectangle. Reapply the 20 mm and 25 mm **Constraints** selecting the 2 limiting lines instead of the line length.)

7) Use procedures similar, re-constrain and apply a **Chamfer** to the lower left corner of the sketch of length **10 mm** and angle **45°**.

8) **Exit** the Sketcher and

Pocket the sketch using the option **Up to Last**.

9) **Propagate**

Chapter 2: SKETCHER

Tutorial 2.5: Axes & Transformations

FEATURED TOPICS & COMMANDS

AXES 2

THE TRANSFORMATION TOOLBAR 2

TUTORIAL 2.5 START 3

    Section 1: Using Axes 3

    Section 2: Transformations...6

PREREQUISITE KNOWLEDGE & COMMANDS

- Entering workbenches.
- Entering and exiting the *Sketcher* workbench
- Work modes (*Sketch tools* toolbar)
- Creating profiles
- Applying dimensional and geometric constraints
- Editing a preexisting sketch
- Simple pads and pockets
- Rotating the part using the mouse or compass

AXES

An axis is a line of symmetry. The *Axis* command is located in the *Profile* toolbar. When an axis line is draw it is automatically drawn as a construction element. Therefore, it does not become part of the final sketch. Axes are often used to facilitate the drawing process when using commands such as *Mirror*. It may also be used as the rotation axis when creating a *Shaft* (a revolved solid) or a *Groove* in the *Part Design* workbench.

THE TRANSFORMATION TOOLBAR

Transformation tools allow you to change, or create an array of a sketch. These tools allow you to use an existing sketch to define a new sketch that is a mirror image, a rotated version, or a different size from the original sketch. Many of the transformation commands may be used in 'duplicate' mode which enables arrays to be created. The *Transformation* toolbar in located in the *Operation* toolbar. Reading from left to right, the *Transformation* toolbar contains the following commands

- Mirror: The *Mirror* command creates a mirror image of a sketch about a selected axis.
- Symmetry: The *Symmetry* command replaces a sketch with its mirror image.
- Translate: The *Translate* command moves a sketch from one point to another. This command may be used in duplicate mode to create a linear array.
- Rotate: The *Rotate* command rotates a sketch around a selected center point. This command may be used in duplicate mode to create a polar array.
- Scale: The *Scale* command scales a sketch relative to a selected point. This command may be used in duplicate mode which creates several instances of the sketch.
- Offset: The *Offset* command creates a sketch that is offset from the original by a specified distance. This command scales and adjusts the sketch as appropriate. Given the complex nature of this command, it does not always work as intended.

TUTORIAL 2.5 START

The part modeled in this tutorial is shown on the right. The outside hub is created using an *Axis* and the *Shaft* command. The spokes are created using the *Rotate* command, and the triangular *Pockets* are created using the *Mirror* command.

Section 1: Using Axes

1) Start a **New 3D Part** and name it **T25Wheel**.

2) Make your **PartBody** the **In Work Object**.

3) Enter the **Sketcher** on the **yz plane**.

4) Draw an **Axis** that is on and aligned with the vertical (V) axis.

5) Draw and **Constrain** the **Profile** shown. Depending on how many geometric constraints were applied, you may or may not have to include all of the dimensional constraints shown. The sketch should be iso-constrained when complete.

6) **Exit** the Sketcher and **Shaft** the sketch using the Sketch Axis as the rotation axis. In the *Shaft Definition* window fill in the following fields;

- First angle: *360*
- Second angle: *0*
- Profile Selection: **Sketch.1**
- Axis Selection: **Sketch Axis**

7) In the *Part Design* workbench apply fillets to the inside corners of the hub. Select the **Edge Fillet** icon. In the *Edge Fillet Definition* window, set the fillet radius to *2 mm*. Activate the *object(s) to fillet:* field and select all 6 inside edges and then select **OK**.

Edges to fillet.
(Same edges on the other side.)

8) Deselect all and enter the **Sketcher** on the **yz plane**.

9) Select the **Cut Part by Sketch Plane** icon located in the *Visualization* toolbar usually in the top toolbar area.

10) Draw an **Axis** that is on and aligned with the V axis.

11) Draw and **Constrain** the **Profile** shown.

12) **Exit** the Sketcher and **Shaft** the sketch **360** degrees using the Sketch Axis as the rotation axis.

13) **Propagate**.

Section 2: Transformations

1) Check to see if your *Reference Element (Extended)* toolbar is active. At the top pull down menu select **View – Toolbars**. A check mark should be next to **Reference Elements (Extended)**. If there is not check mark, select it. If it is not apparent where this toolbar is, look in the bottom right corner for any hidden toolbars.

2) Create a new sketch plane by offsetting the xy plane by 12 mm. Select the **Plane**

    icon. In the *Plane Definition* window fill in the following fields;
   - `Plane type`: **Offset from plane**
   - `Reference`: right click and select **xy plane**
   - `Offset`: *12 mm*.

   Then select **OK**. A new plane should be created 12 mm from the xy plane.

3) Enter the **Sketcher** on the newly created plane.

4) Pull out the *Transformation* subtoolbar.

5) Draw and **Constrain** 🔲 the following **Ellipse** ⬭. To constrain the major axis just click on the ellipse. To constrain the minor axis click on the ellipse, when the major axis dimension appears, right click and select **Semiminor axis**.

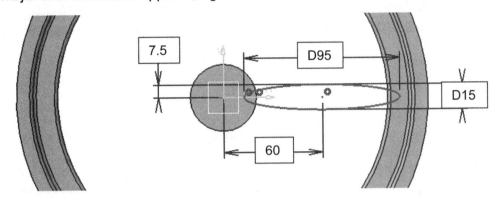

(**Problem?** If your ellipse went on an angle after you adjusted your dimensions, add an angular dimension between the H axis and the ellipse.)

6) Array the ellipse to create a total of 8 ellipses each 45 degrees apart. Select the ellipse and then select the

Rotate 🔄 icon. In the *Rotation Definition* window select **7** Instance(s), and activate the **Duplicate mode**. Notice that the Angle field does not allow you to enter a value yet. Look at the *Status Bar*. Select the center point to be the coordinate origin, enter an angle of **45deg** and then select **OK**.

7) **Exit** the Sketcher and **Pad** the sketch to a length of *11 mm*.

8) **Propagate**.

9) Select the **Edge Fillet** icon. In the *Edge Fillet Definition* window, set the fillet radius to *2 mm*. With the object(s) to fillet: field active select all 16 side faces of the padded ellipsis and then select **OK**.

Side faces

10) Enter the **Sketcher** ![icon] on the top face of the center hub.

Sketch face

11) Draw and **Constrain** ![icon] the following **Axis** ![icon] and **Profile** ![icon].

12) Use the *Symmetry* command to mirror the original sketch to the other side of the axis. Select all elements of the triangle, select the **Symmetry** ![icon] icon and then select the axis.

13) On your own, use the **Mirror** ![icon] command to create a copy of the sketch on the other side of the axis.

14) **Rotate** both triangles through a distance of **90deg** creating **1** instance in the **Duplicate mode**.

15) **Exit** the Sketcher and **Pocket** the sketch using the option **Up to last**.

(**Problems?** If your sketch disappears, *Copy* and *Paste* the Sketch as described in the preface.)

16) **Propagate**

Chapter 2: SKETCHER

Tutorial 2.6: Operations on 3D Geometries & Sketch planes

FEATURED TOPICS & COMMANDS

THE 3D GEOMETRY TOOLBAR 2

THE REFERENCE ELEMENT TOOLBAR...2

TUTORIAL 2.6 START 3

    Section 1: 3D Project Elements 3

    Section 2: Project 3D Silhouette Edges..7

    Section 3: Intersect 3D Elements. 11

PREREQUISITE KNOWLEDGE & COMMANDS

- Entering workbenches
- Entering and exiting the *Sketcher* workbench
- Work modes (*Sketch tools* toolbar)
- Creating profiles
- Applying dimensional and geometric constraints
- Editing a preexisting sketch
- Simple pads and pockets
- Rotating the part using the mouse or compass

THE 3D GEOMETRY TOOLBAR

Many times it is necessary to relate the current sketch to the existing solid part. There are two ways of doing this. You can constrain the sketch using the edges of the part as a point of reference, or you can project the part's edges and silhouettes onto the sketch plane. This second method of projection has many advantages. It is quick (you don't have to redraw the sketch) and the projection is associative. An associative projected sketch is connected to the existing part and automatically updates when the part is changed. The default color of an associative sketch is yellow. The *3D Geometry* toolbar is located in the *Operation* toolbar. The commands in the *3D Geometry* toolbar from left to right are

- Project 3D Elements: This command allows you to project edges of the solid part onto the sketch plane.
- Intersect 3D Elements: This command allows you to project the intersection between the part and the sketch plane.
- Project 3D Silhouette Edges: This command allows you to create a silhouette of the solid part. You can only create a silhouette edge projection from a surface of revolution whose axis is parallel to the sketch plane.
- Project 3D Canconical Silhouette Edges: This command allows you to create a silhouette of a surface of revolution whose axis is parallel to the sketch plane.
- Isolate: *Isolate* is a command that is not located in the *3D Geometry* toolbar but is used in conjunction with the above three commands. *Isolate* breaks the link between the projected sketch and the part. Once the *Isolate* command has been applied to a sketch, the sketch will no longer be associative. To access this command select *Insert – Operation – 3D Geometry – Isolate*.

THE REFERENCE ELEMENT TOOLBAR

Thus far our sketch planes have mainly been the 3 principle planes or a face of the part. Many times we need a sketch plane that cannot be defined by the original coordinate system or the part. The commands located in the *Reference Element* toolbar allows us to create planes and other reference elements that may be used as the sketch plane or help in the creation of a sketch plane. These elements are not standard elements and will not become part of your solid. The *Reference Element* toolbar is located in the *Part Design* workbench. If it is not active, select *View – Toolbars – Reference Elements (Extended)*. The commands located in the *Reference Element* toolbar from left to right are

- Point: Allows you to create a reference point.
- Line: Allows you to create a reference line. Mainly used to define a direction for another command.
- Plane: Used to create a reference plane to be used as a sketch plane. There are many ways to create a reference plane. A couple examples include; a plane offset from an existing plane or part face, and a plane at an angle to another plane of part face.

TUTORIAL 2.6 START

The part modeled in this tutorial is shown on the right. This part is constructed using projections and reference planes. Notice that several reference planes have been created to facilitate the drawing process.

Section 1: 3D Project Elements

1) Open a **New 3D Part** and name it *T26Channel*.

2) Make your **PartBody** the **In Work Object** and change your **Units** to **Millimeters**.

3) Enter the **Sketcher** on the **yz plane**.

4) Draw and **Constrain** the following **Profile** and **Circle** shown. Notice that the circle's center is coincident with the origin.

5) **Exit** the *Sketcher* and **Pad** the sketch to a length of **20 mm**.

Projected element

Offset element

6) Create a reference plane that is offset from the yz plane by 100 mm. If the *Reference Element (Extended)* toolbar is not active, activate it (It may be hidden in the bottom right corner). At the top pull down menu select **View** – **Toolbars** – **Reference**

Elements (Extended). Select the **Plane** icon. In the *Plane Definition* window fill in the following fields;
- Plane type: **Offset from plane**
- Reference: right click and select **yz plane**
- Offset: **100 mm**.

7) Enter on the **Sketcher** on the newly created plane.

8) Select the **Isometric View** icon.

Project

Offset plane

9) Display the **Grid** .

10) Use the **3D Project Elements** to project the outline of the hole onto the sketch plane. Notice that the projection is yellow. This means that it is associated with the part.

11) Offset the projection 10 mm to the inside. Select the **Offset** icon (located in the *Transformation* toolbar), select the projection, and then enter an Offset of **-10 mm** in the value field.

Sketch tools						
	New Position: H: 32.922mm	V: -38.556mm	Offset: -10			Instance(s): 1

12) Draw a horizontal **Line** between quadrants of the outside projected circle.

13) Use the **Quick Trim** command to trim off the top half of the two circles as well as the portion of the line inside the smaller circle. The trimmed portions of the associated elements will turn into construction elements.

Trimmed

14) **Exit** the *Sketcher* and **Pad** the sketch to a length of **180 mm** in the **Reverse Direction**.

15) **Propagate**.

16) Edit Sketch.1.

17) Change the hole diameter to **40 mm**.

18) **Exit** the *Sketcher.* Notice that Pad.2 which is based on the projection updates automatically.

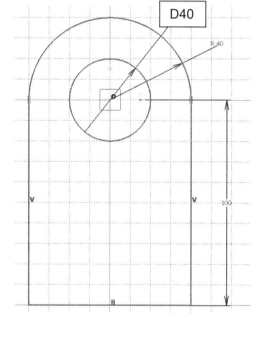

19) Edit Sketch.2.

20) Use a selection window to select all the elements in Sketch.2. Then at the top pull down menu, select **Insert – Operation – 3D Geometry – Isolate**. Notice that the projections are no longer yellow. They are not associated with the part anymore.

21) **Exit** the *Sketcher* and edit Sketch.1.

22) Change the Sketch.1 hole diameter back to *60 mm*.

23) **Exit** the *Sketcher*. Notice that Pad.2 does not update this time.

Section 2: Project 3D Silhouette Edges

1) Offset a **Plane** *10 mm* from the **yz plane**.

2) Enter on the **Sketcher** on the newly created plane.

3) Draw and constrain the following Sketch.

4) **Exit** the *Sketcher* and **Shaft** the sketch through ***360deg*** using the **V Direction** as the rotation axis. To select the V Direction, activate the `Selection:` field and select the V axis on the part.

5) Offset a **Plane** *100 mm* from the **zx plane**.

6) Enter on the **Sketcher** on the newly created plane.

7) Select the **Fit All In** and the **Isometric View** icons.

8) Try using **3D Project Elements** to project the Shafted sphere. You can't do it. All you get is a point. Delete the point that was created.

9) Use **Project 3D Canonical Silhouette Edges** to project the silhouette of the two protruding parts of the sphere.

10) Draw **Lines** to connect the top ends and bottoms ends of the projected arcs.

11) Delete the parallel constraint between the two lines if one appears.

12) **Exit** the *Sketcher* and **Pad** the sketch to a length of *100 mm* in the **Reverse Direction**.

(**Problems?** If CATIA will not allow you to Pad your sketch, you may not have deleted the point in the middle of the sketch. Edit the sketch and turn the point into a Construction Element.)

13) Edit Sketch.3. This is the sketch associated with the *Shaft*.

14) Change the radius dimension to *25 mm*.

15) **Exit** the *Sketcher*. Notice that Pad.3 automatically updates.

R25

Section 3: Intersect 3D Elements.

1) Create two reference points. Select the **Point**
   icon.   In the *Point Definition* window fill in the
   following fields;
   - Point type: **On curve**
   - Curve: select the top line shown in the figure
   - Distance to reference: activate **Ratio of curve length**
   - Ratio: *0.5*.
   - Point: Clear the selection
   Create a second point on the bottom line in a similar
   fashion.

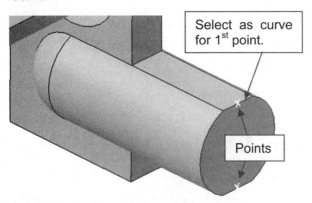

Select as curve for 1st point.

Points

2) Create a reference **Line**
   between the two
   points.

3) Select the **Plane** icon. In the *Plane Definition* window fill in the following fields;
- Plane type: **Angle/Normal to plane**
- Rotation axis: click on the **Line.1** (the reference line)
- Reference: select the surface indicated in the figure
- Angle: *30deg*.

Reference surface

4) Enter on the **Sketcher** on the newly created plane.

5) Select the **Isometric View** icon.

6) Select the **Intersect 3D Elements** icon. Then select Pad.3 (the last pad) in the specification tree.

16) **Exit** the *Sketcher* and **Pad** the sketch to a length of *50 mm* in the **Reverse Direction**.

17) **Propagate**

Chapter 2: SKETCHER

Tutorial 2.7: Points & Splines

FEATURED TOPICS & COMMANDS

POINTS 2

SPLINES 2

TUTORIAL 2.7 START 3

    Section 1: Entering points. 4

    Section 2: Creating and editing splines. 5

PREREQUISITE KNOWLEDGE & COMMANDS

- Entering workbenches
- Entering and exiting the *Sketcher* workbench
- Work modes (*Sketch tools* toolbar)
- Creating profiles
- Applying dimensional and geometric constraints
- Editing a preexisting sketch
- Simple pads and pockets
- Rotating the part using the mouse or compass

POINTS

Points are used to define some aspects of 2D geometries. For instance, a line is defined by two end points, and a circle is defined by a center point and a radius. When creating geometries such as lines, circles, rectangles and profiles, points are automatically created by CATIA. However, points may also be created by the user. User created points are used when creating splines and wireframes. The *Point* sub-toolbar is located within the *Profile* toolbar. Reading from left to right, the *Point* sub-toolbar contains the following commands

- Point by Clicking: Allows you to create a point by clicking anywhere on the screen. The position of this point may be changed later by double clicking on and entering a new position in the *Point Definition* window.
- Point by Using Coordinates: Allows you to create a point by entering a Cartesian or polar coordinate in the *Point Definition* window.
- Equidistant Points: Allows you to create a specified number of equidistant points along a previously drawn curve.
- Intersection Point: Allows you to create a point at the intersection of two elements.
- Projection Point: Projects (in 2D) a point onto a pre-existing profile. The projection line which connects the point with the profile creates a 90° angle with the profile.

SPLINES

Splines are used when a profile is curved and complex. Such profiles are too complex and are difficult to create using arcs and conics. Reading from left to right, the *Spline* toolbar contains the following commands.

- Spline: A spline is a curved profile defined by three or more points. The tangency and curvature radius at each point may be specified.
- Connect: The connect command connects two points or profiles with a spline.

TUTORIAL 2.7 START

The part modeled in this tutorial is a cam. The cam profile is created by using construction points and a spline. The cam profile is then modified by entering the *Spline Definition* window and adding and modifying the points used to create the spline. The cam is shown at two different stages of the tutorial. The original cam profile is shown below. The cam profile graph shows the follower's displacement versus the rotation angle. The cam has a base circle radius of 1.5 inches.

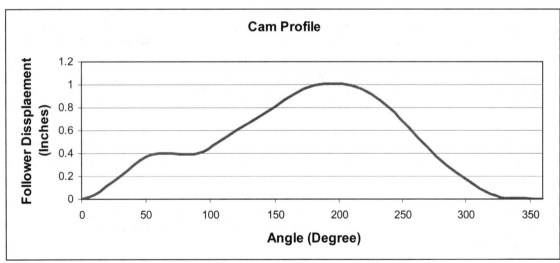

Section 1: Entering points.

1) Start a **New 3D Part** name it *T27Cam* and, make your **PartBody** the **In Work Object**, change your **units** to **inches**, and enter the **Sketcher** on the **yz plane**.

2) At the top pull down menu, select **Tools – Options...** Deactivate the grid display and snap to point options. In the left side menu of the *Options* window, select **Parameters and Measure**. Click on the **Units** tab and set the length units to **Inches**.

3) Activate the **Construction/Standard Element** icon. We want the points that we will be creating to be construction elements.

4) <u>Double click</u>* on the **Point by Using Coordinate** icon. In the *Point Definition* window click on the **Polar** tab and enter a radius of *1.5in* and an Angle of *0deg*. Then select **OK**. When the next *Point Definition* window appears, click on the **Polar** tab and enter a radius of *1.7in* and an Angle of *30deg*. Continue filling in the *Point Definition* window with the following Cam profile data. Remember to add the base circle radius to each displacement point. We have already entered the first two points. Start with the third.

* Double clicking allows you to continually enter points that are relative to the origin. If you don't double click you will end up entering points that are relative to the last point created unless you deselect the last point each time.

Angle (Degrees)	Follower Displacement (Inches)
0	0
30	0.2
60	0.4
90	0.4
105	0.49
120	0.6
135	0.705
150	0.81
165	0.92
180	1
210	1
225	0.92
240	0.79
255	0.62
270	0.45
285	0.3
300	0.18
315	0.07
330	0.01

Section 2: Creating and editing splines.

1) Deselect all and then deactivate the **Construction/Standard Element** icon.

2) Click on the **Spline** icon. Move your mouse to the first created point (1.5in<0deg). When a bull's-eye symbol appears click. Select each successive point until you return to the first point. Double click on the first point to end the spline.

Bull's-eye symbol

3) **Exit** the *Sketcher* and **Pad** the sketch to a length of *.25in* in both directions (**Mirrored extent**).

(**Problems?** If CATIA does not allow you to pad the spline, one of the points used to create the spline may be a standard element instead of a construction element.)

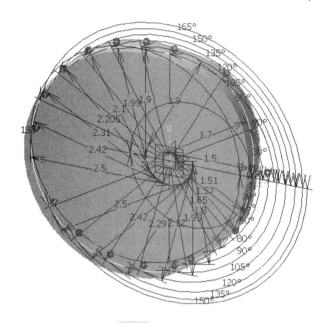

4) Enter the **Sketcher** on the **yz plane**.

5) Draw a **Circle** that is centered at the origin and has a diameter of *1.25 in*.

6) **Exit** the *Sketcher* and **Pad** the sketch to a length of *1in* in both directions (**Mirrored extent**).

7) Enter the **Sketcher** on the front face of the center hub.

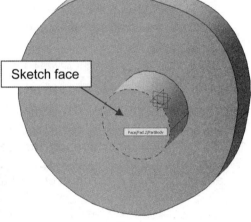

Sketch face

8) Draw and constrain the following sketch.

.125

.061

.35

D.5

9) **Exit** the *Sketcher* and **Pocket** the sketch using the option **Up to last**.

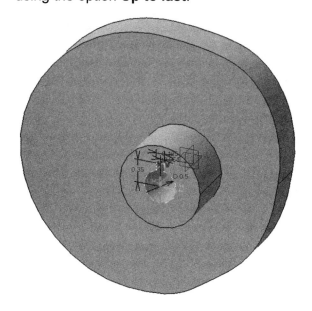

10) **Propagate**.

11) Edit Sketch.1.

12) Double click anywhere on the spline. In the *Spline Definition* window, click on **CtrPoint.4** and activate **Replace Point**. Click on the graphics screen somewhere above CtrPoint.4 making sure not to create any constraints. Click **OK**.

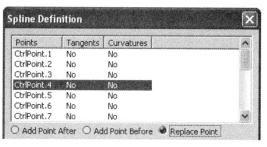

13) Double click on the newly created point. In the *Point Definition* window, click on the **Polar** tab and enter a radius of *2.1in* and an angle of *90deg*.

14) Double click on the spline. In the *Spline Definition* window click on **CtrlPoint.3** and activate **Add Point After**. Click somewhere between CtrlPoint.3 and CtrlPoint.4 making sure not to create any constraints.

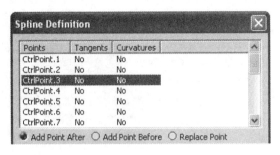

15) Edit the new point's position and enter R = *2in* and A = *80deg*.

16) Double click on the spline. In the *Spline Definition* window click on **CtrlPoint.21** the point between CtrlPoint.3 and CtrlPoint.4. Activate both the **Tangency** and **Curvature Radius** toggles. Enter a Curvature Radius of *.4in*. Look at the spline while you click **OK** to see the effect that changing the curvature radius has on the spline.

17) **Exit** the *Sketcher.*

18) Change the diameter of inner hub from 1.25 inches to *1 inch.*

19) **Propagate**.

Exercise 2.1: This exercise can be performed after completing tutorial 2.1. Model the following parts using the *Snap to Point* command to estimate distances. You will be creating a 3-D models based on the 2-D orthographic projections shown.

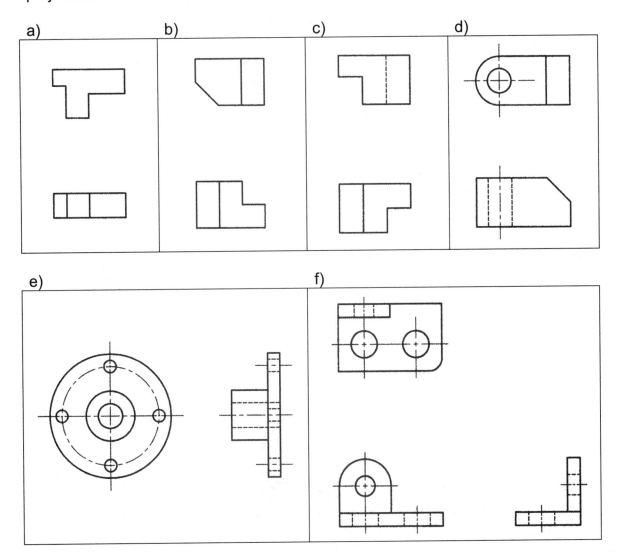

Exercise 2.2: This exercise can be performed after completing tutorial 2.2. Model the following parts applying the appropriate constraints. To set the appropriate units, select *Tools – Options... – Parameters and Measure*.

a)

b)

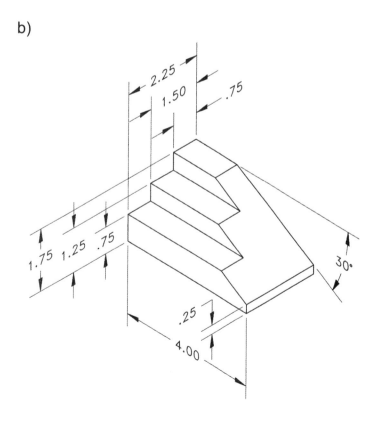

Exercise 2.3: This exercise can be performed after completing tutorial 2.3. Model the following parts applying the appropriate constraints. To set the appropriate units, select _Tools_ – _Options... – Parameters and Measure._

a)

b)

c)

d)

Exercise 2.4: This exercise can be performed after completing tutorial 2.4. Sketch the following parts applying the appropriate constraints. To set the appropriate units, select _Tools_ – _Options..._ – _Parameters and Measure_.

a)

b)

Exercise 2.5: This exercise can be performed after completing tutorial 2.5. Model the following parts applying the appropriate constraints, and transformations during the sketch phase. Use at least one transformation command to create the object. To set the appropriate units, select _Tools – Options... – Parameters and Measure._

a)

b)

Exercise 2.6: This exercise can be performed after completing tutorial 2.6. Model the following parts applying the appropriate constraints, and using reference elements and projections where necessary. To set the appropriate units, select _Tools_ – _Options..._ – _Parameters and Measure_.

a)

b)

Chapter 3: PART DESIGN

INTRODUCTION

Chapter 3 focuses on CATIA's *Part Design* workbench. The reader will learn how to use sketches to create solids and how to create solids without the aid of sketches.

TUTORIALS CONTAINED IN CHAPTER 3

- Tutorial 3.1: Sketch-Based Features: Pads
- Tutorial 3.2: Sketch-Based Features: Pockets, Holes & Slots
- Tutorial 3.3: Sketch-Based Features: Shafts & Grooves
- Tutorial 3.4: Sketch-Based Features: Advanced commands
- Tutorial 3.5: Dress-Up Features: Drafts, Fillets & Chamfers
- Tutorial 3.6: Dress-Up Features: Shell, Thickness & Threads
- Tutorial 3.7: Transformation Features
- Tutorial 3.8: Boolean Operations
- Tutorial 3.9: Material Properties

NOTES:

Chapter 3:
PART DESIGN

Tutorial 3.1: Sketch-Based Features: Pads

FEATURED TOPICS & COMMANDS

THE PART DESIGN WORKBENCH 2

THE SKETCH-BASED FEATURES TOOLBAR 2

THE PADS TOOLBAR 3

TUTORIAL 3.1 START 4

    Section 1: Creating Multi-Pads 4

    Section 2: Advanced Pads 7

    Section 3: Creating Drafted Filleted Pads 15

PREREQUISITE KNOWLEDGE & COMMANDS

- The *Sketcher* workbench and associated commands
- Editing a preexisting sketch
- Simple pads and pockets
- Rotating the part using the mouse or compass

THE PART DESIGN WORKBENCH

The *Part Design* workbench is used to create and modify solids. A solid is first created using an initial sketch. Once the main solid is created, it may be modified using sketch based feature commands or using commands that do not require a sketch. The general design process is to; sketch the profile of the main pad, generate the main pad, create additional sketch based features, add dress-up features, modify features as desired, and insert new bodies for more complex parts.

THE SKETCH-BASED FEATURES TOOLBAR

The commands located in the *Sketch-Based Features* toolbar use sketches to create or modify a solid. Therefore, to modify the shape of the feature, the sketch must first be modified. The depth, length of travel, rotation angle, etc... may be modified in the respective definition windows. It is possible to modify a feature (Pad, Pocket, etc...) after it has been created. Just double click on the respective feature in the specification tree and the *Definition* window will appear allowing you to change the parameters. Reading left to right, the commands in the *Sketch-Based Features* toolbar are

- Pad: *Pads* are used to add or create solid material in a linear direction.
- Pocket: *Pockets* are used to remove material in a linear direction.
- Shaft: *Shafts* are used to add or create material by revolving a sketch about an axis.

- Groove: *Grooves* are used to remove material by revolving a sketch about an axis.
- Hole: The *Hole* command is used to create holes of different configurations. For example, this command could be used to create a simple blind hole or a more complex counter bore and drilled hole, or even a threaded hole.
- Rib: The *Rib* command is used to add material by sweeping a profile along a center curve.
- Slot: *Slots* are used to remove material by sweeping a profile along a center curve.
- Advanced Sketch-Based Features toolbar: This toolbar contains the commands, *Solid Combine* and *Stiffener*. *Stiffener* is used to create relatively thin supporting structures for your part.
- Multi-sections Solid: *Multi-sections Solid* is used to create or add material by connecting several sketches.
- Remove Multi-sections Solid: *Remove Multi-sections Solid* is used to remove material by connecting several sketches.

THE PADS TOOLBAR

The *Pads* toolbar, along with the simple *Pad* command, contains advanced commands for creating pads. The *Pads* toolbar reading from left to right contains the following commands.

- Pad: This command is used to create a simple pad.
- Drafted Filleted Pad: This command is used to create a pad that has angled sides and rounded edges.
- Multi-Pad: This command is used to create pads of varying depth all within a single sketch.

TUTORIAL 3.1 START

The part modeled in this tutorial is shown on the right. The entire part is created exclusively using the commands located in the *Pads* toolbar and their supportive sketches.

Section 1: Creating Multi-Pads

1) Start a **New 3D Part** and name is **T31Pad** and make your **PartBody** the **In Work Object**.

2) Enter the **Sketcher** on the **xy plane**. Deactivate the Grid's Snap to Point and Display.

3) Before you start to draw make sure your length units are set to millimeters. (**Tools – Options... – Parameters and Measures**)

4) Draw and **Constrain** the following **Rectangle**.

5) **Exit** the *Sketcher.*

6) Pull out the *Pads* toolbar .

7) **Pad** the sketch to a length of **20 mm**. Select **OK**. In the specification tree, double click on Pad.1. The Pad Definition window will appear. If needed you could change the pad features. Select **Cancel**.

8) Enter the **Sketcher** on the top face of the block.

9) **3D Project Elements** the face of the block on to the sketch plane as a **Construction Element**.

Why? Why are we using construction elements? The construction elements projected in the previous step will help us locate the Rectangles created in the next steps. We will snap the Rectangles to the construction element. You know that you have snapped the Rectangle to the construction element if you create a coincident constrain .

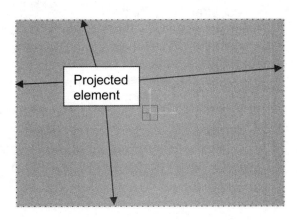

10) Draw and **Constrain** the following **Rectangles**. Make sure to snap exactly to the corner. Add enough constrain to create an iso-constrained (green) sketch.

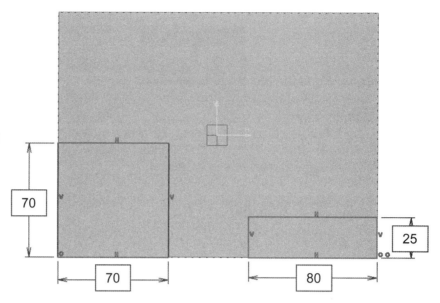

11) Add the following **Profiles** to the sketch. Make sure not to draw overlapping lines.

(**Problem?**

- Is your sketch <u>over constrained</u> (pink)? Look at the coincident constraints. These are usually the culprit. CATIA may create a coincident constraint between two distance corners. Delete this constraint and see if the sketch becomes iso-constrained (green).)
- If your sketch moves off of the projection, use dimensions (value = 0) to move it back on. You can't dimension to a group projection so you will have to either dimension to the bottom surface or hide the projection temporarily.)

12) **Exit** the Sketcher and select the **Multi-Pad** icon. In the *Multi-Pad Definition* window click on one of the *Extrusion domains* in the Domains field. Notice that a feature will highlight in blue on the part. Type in that feature's length and click on the next, etc... The pad lengths are as follows. The lone rectangle is **5 mm**, the corner rectangle in the group of three is **10 mm**, the next is **20 mm**, and the last is **30 mm**.

Sketch face

13) **Propagate**.

Section 2: Advanced Pads

2-1: Adding and removing elements of a sketch.

CATIA allows you to *Pad* only a portion of a sketch. The user may manually add or remove elements from the profile definition.

1) Enter the **Sketcher** on the top face of the main pad as shown in the figure above.

2) **3D Project Elements** the top face of the main pad on to the sketch plane as a **Construction Element**.

Why? Just like before, we are projecting the construction elements to help locate the profiles created in the next step. We will snap the profile to the construction element and obtain the coincident constraints.

3) Draw the two **Profiles** shown in the figure. The dimensions of the small rectangle is not important.

4) **Exit** the Sketcher and deselect all.

5) Select the **Pad** icon. In the *Pad Definition* window, right click on the `Selection:` field and click on **Go to profile definition**. In the *Profile Definition* window, activate the **Sub-element** toggle

and click the **Add** button and select the profile indicated in the figure. Select **OK**. In the *Pad Definition* window, set the length to *30 mm* and apply the pad.

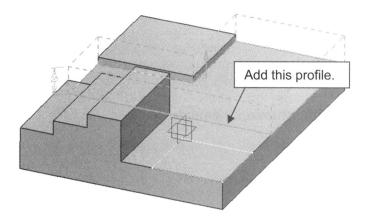

Add this profile.

2-2: Padding using an open profile.

CATIA allows you to *Pad* an open profile as long as it is bounded by the part.

1) Right click on **Sketch.3** (the last sketch) in the specification tree and select **Hide/Show**.

2) Enter the **Sketcher** on the top face of the main pad.

Sketch face

3) **3D Project Elements** the top face of the main pad on to the sketch plane as a **Construction Element**.

4) Draw and **Constrain** the closed **Profile** shown in the figure.

5) **Exit** the *Sketcher* and **Pad** the sketch to a length of **30 mm**.

6) Enter the **Sketcher** on the top face of the main pad.

Sketch face

7) **3D Project Elements** the top face of the main pad on to the sketch plane as a **Construction Element**.

8) Draw a **Spline** similar to that shown in the figure.

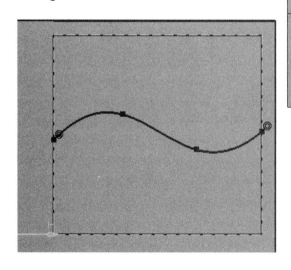

9) **Exit** the *Sketcher* and select the **Pad** icon. Set the length to **20 mm** and select the **Preview** button. Select the **Reverse Side** button and **Preview** again (you may have to click on the screen to reactivate the preview button). Notice the difference. Apply the *Pad* when it looks like the figure.

10) **Propagate**.

2-3: Padding to a surface.

CATIA allows you to *Pad* up to a surface or offset from the surface. If an offset option is used, the end of the *Pad* takes on the same shape as the surface.

1) Rotate the part and enter the **Sketcher** on the face indicated in the figure.

Sketch face

2) **3D Project Elements** the sketch face on to the sketch plane as a **Construction Element**.

3) Draw and **Constrain** the followir
coincident (the same) and the
constraint may be applied after tl

75

R110

R100

100

Centers are
coincident

0

10

4) **Exit** the *Sketcher* and **Pad** the sketch to a length of
120 mm. You may have to reverse the direction.

Pad Definition

First Limit

Type: Dimension

Length: 120mm

Limit: No selection

Profile/Surface

Selection: Sketch.6

☐ Thick

Reverse Side

☐ Mirrored extent

Reverse Direction

More>>

OK   Cancel   Preview

75

R 110

R 100

100

Sketch face

10

5) Enter the **Sketcher** on the top flat face of the part.

6) **Cut Part By Sketch Plane** .

7) **3D Project Elements** the sketch face on to the sketch plane as a **Construction Element**.

8) Draw and **Constrain** the **Rectangle** shown in the figure.

9) **Exit** the Sketcher and **Pad** the sketch using the option of **Up to surface**. Activate the Limit: field and select the surface indicated in the figure and set the Offset: to *-10 mm*.

10) **Propagate**.

Limit surface

2-4: Padding with thickness.

CATIA gives you the option of padding a sketch with thickness. In simple terms, it means that you can easily create a thin walled section.

1) Rotate the part and enter the **Sketcher** on the face indicated in the figure.

2) **3D Project Elements** the left edge the sketch face on to the sketch plane as a **Construction Element**.

Sketch face

Face/Pad.2/PartBody

3) Draw and **Constrain** the **Rectangle** shown in the figure.

25

30

30

4) **Exit** the Sketcher and select the **Pad** icon. Set the length to be *120 mm* and select the **More>>** button. On the left side of the window, activate the **Thick** toggle. On the right side of the window enter a value of *2 mm* for Thickness 1.

Sketch face

Section 3: Creating Drafted Filleted Pads

1) Enter the **Sketcher** on the right face of the part as shown in the figure above.

2) Draw and **Constrain** the **Rectangle** shown in the figure.

3) Exit the Sketcher and select the **Drafted Filleted Pad** icon. Set the Length: to be *50 mm*. Activate the Limit: Field and select the sketch face. The draft angle is *5deg* and all the fillets are *5 mm*.

Drafted Filleted Pad Definition	? X
First Limit	
Length:	50mm
Second Limit	
Limit:	Pad.7\Face.2
Draft	
Angle:	5deg
Neutral element:	● First limit ○ Second limit
Fillets	
Lateral radius:	5mm
First limit radius:	5mm
Second limit radius:	5mm
Reverse Direction	
OK	Cancel	Preview

4) **Propagate**.

Chapter 3: PART DESIGN

Tutorial 3.2: Sketch-Based Features: Pockets, Holes & Slots

FEATURED TOPICS & COMMANDS

THE POCKETS TOOLBAR 2

HOLES 2

SLOTS 2

TUTORIAL 3.2 START 3

    Section 1: Creating Pockets 3

    Section 2: Creating Slots. 7

    Section 3: Creating Holes. 9

PREREQUISITE KNOWLEDGE & COMMANDS

- The *Sketcher* workbench and associated commands
- Editing a preexisting sketch
- Pads
- Rotating the part using the mouse or compass

THE POCKETS TOOLBAR

The *Pockets* toolbar, along with the simple *Pocket* command, contains advanced commands for creating pockets. The *Pockets* toolbar, reading from left to right, contains the following commands.

- Pocket: This command is used to create a simple pocket.
- Drafted Filleted Pocket: This command is used to create a pocket that has angled sides and rounded edges.
- Multi-Pocket: This command is used to create pockets of varying depth all within a single sketch.

HOLES

The *Hole* command (located in the *Sketch Based Features* toolbar) is used to create holes of different configurations. For example, this command could be used to create a simple blind hole or a more complex counter bore and drilled hole, or even a threaded hole. The *Hole* command is initiated in the *Part Design* workbench without a preexisting sketch. However, the command automatically creates a sketch; therefore, it is still a sketch based feature.

SLOTS

The *Slot* command (located in the *Sketch Based Features* toolbar) is used to remove material by sweeping a profile along a center curve. The profile may be opened or closed depending on the options chosen. The center curve should not be made of multiple geometric elements.

TUTORIAL 3.2 START

The part modeled in this tutorial is shown on the right. It is created from one main pad and then modified using the *Pocket, Hole* and *Slot* commands. Several different *Pocket* and *Hole* options are explored.

Section 1: Creating Pockets

1) Start a **New 3D Part** and name it *T32Pockets*, set your **units** to **millimeters**, make your **PartBody** the **In Work Object** and enter the **Sketcher** on the **xy plane**..

2) Draw and **Constrain** the following **Rectangle**.

3) **Exit** the *Sketcher* and **Pad** the sketch to a length of **80 mm**.

4) Enter the **Sketcher** on the top face of the block.

5) Draw and **Constrain** the following sketch. All the **Corner** (fillet) radii are **5 mm** and all the hole diameters are **15 mm**. To avoid unwanted constrains, hold the **SHIFT** key down when drawing the circles.

6) **Exit** the *Sketcher* and then pull out the **Pockets** toolbar

7) **Propagate**.

8) Select the **Multi-Pocket** icon. Set the depth of the inside holes to *80 mm* and the depth of the outside profile to be *10 mm*. Remember when you click on one of the Extrusion domains it will highlight the respective feature on the part.

9) Enter the **Sketcher** on the left face of the part as shown in the figure.

10) **3D Project Elements** the sketch face on to the sketch plane as a **Construction Element**.

11) Deactivate the **Standard/Construction Element** icon. **Offset** the projection by *-15 mm*. The offset rectangle should be a **Standard Element**.

12) **Exit** the *Sketcher* and select the

Pocket icon. In the *Pocket Definition* window, select the **More>>** button. Activate the **Thick** toggle. Set the pocket depth to be **20 mm** and both thickness' to be **3 mm**. Set and preview one thickness at a time to see which direction is effected by both.

13) Enter the **Sketcher** on the left face of the part.

14) **3D Project Elements** the inside portion of the sketch face on to the sketch plane as a **Construction Element**.

15) Draw a **Spline** similar to the one shown in the figure.

16) **Exit** the *Sketcher* and **Pocket** the sketch to a depth of **20 mm**. Use the *Reverse Side* button if necessary to achieve the same results as shown in the figure.

17) **Propagate**.

Section 2: Creating Slots.

1) Enter the **Sketcher** on the top face of the part.

Sketch face

2) **3D Project Elements** the sketch face on to the sketch plane as a **Construction Element**.

3) Draw and **Constrain** a **Standard Element Line** as shown in the figure.

4) **Exit** the *Sketcher* and deselect all.

22.5

75

5) Enter the Sketcher on the right face of the part.

Sketch face

6) **3D Project Elements** the top edge of the sketch face on to the sketch plane as a **Construction Element**.

7) Draw and **Constrain** the following **Profile**. The profile is a closed triangle.

10   25

20   12.5

8) Select the Slot icon. Use the triangle as the Profile: and the line as the Center curve:.

Slot Definition

| Profile | Sketch.6 |
| Center curve | Sketch.5 |

Profile control

Keep angle

Selection: No selection

☐ Move profile to path

☐ Merge slot's ends   ☐ Thick Profile

Thin Slot

Thickness1: 1mm

Thickness2: 0mm

☐ Neutral Fiber ☐ Merge Ends

| OK | Cancel | Preview |

9) **Propagate**.

Section 3: Creating Holes.

1) Select the **Hole** icon and then select the top face of the part. Select the **Extension** tab in the *Hole Definition* window. Create a **Blind** hole with a Diameter: of *10 mm*, a Depth: of *10 mm*, and a **V-Bottom**. Click on the **Positioning Sketch** icon and **Constrain** the center of the hole as shown in the figure.

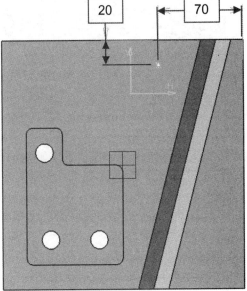

2) **Exit** the *Sketcher* and select **OK**.

3) Create another *20 mm* Diameter: through (**up to last**) **Hole** icon on the top face of the part. The hole should be constrained as shown in the figure.

4) Create a counterbored

Hole with the following parameters. Select the **Type** tab to change the hole type from simple to **Counterbored**.

- Counterbore Diameter: **30 mm**

- Counterbore Depth: **10 mm**.

- Drill Diameter: **20 mm** and it is a through hole.

5) Create a countersunk **Hole**

 with the following parameters.
   - Mode: **Depth & Angle**
   - Countersunk Depth: *10 mm*
   - Angle: *90deg*.
   - Drill Diameter: *20 mm*

   and it is a through hole.

6) **Propagate**.

7) Rotate your part so that the back side is visible.

8) Create a reference line that will control the direction of

a hole. Select the **Line** icon. In the *Line Definition* window, fill in the following fields;
- Line type: **Angle/Normal to curve**
- Curve: Select the bottom edge of the back face
- Point: Select the bottom left corner of the surface
- Support: Select the surface (see fig.)
- Angle: *-45deg*
- Length Type: **Infinite**

Support

Curve
(The bottom edge)

Point
(The corner)

9) Create a **10 deg Tapered**

   through **Hole** on the top face with a **10 mm** diameter that uses the reference line as its direction. To select the direction, deactivate the **Normal to surface** toggle, activate the field below it and

   select the reference line.

10) **Propagate**.

NOTES:

NOTES:

Chapter 3:
PART DESIGN

Tutorial 3.3: Sketch-Based Features: Shafts & Grooves

FEATURED TOPICS & COMMANDS

SHAFTS 2

GROOVES 3

TUTORIAL 3.3 START 4

    Section 1: Creating Shafts. 4

    Section 2: Creating Grooves. 7

PREREQUISITE KNOWLEDGE & COMMANDS

- The *Sketcher* workbench and associated commands
- Editing a preexisting sketch
- Pads
- Rotating the part using the mouse or compass

SHAFTS

A *Shaft* 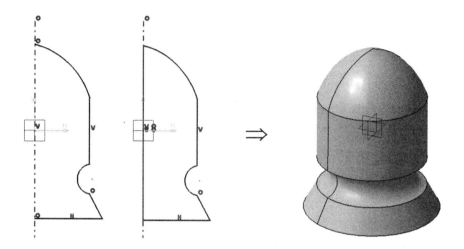 creates a solid by revolving a profile around an axis. Open or closed profiles may be used provided that the profile starts and ends at the axis. Only closed profiles can be used if the profile is away from the axis. The shaft cannot be created if the profile crosses the axis. See the examples shown below.

- Closed or open section may be used when the profile starts and ends on the axis.

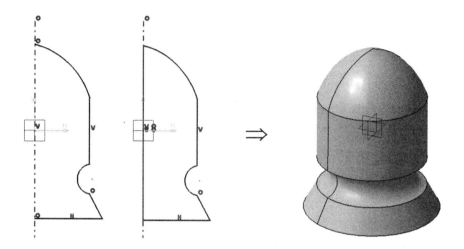

- A closed profile must be used if the sketch does not contact the axis.

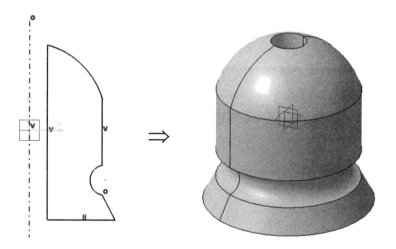

- Profiles that will not produce a shaft.

GROOVES

A *Groove* removes material by revolving a profile around an axis. The profile may be open or closed depending on the options chosen in the *Groove Definition* window. But, the profile should never cross the axis. This command is very similar to the *Shaft* command except that it removes material.

TUTORIAL 3.3 START

The part modeled in this tutorial is shown on the right. The main solid is created using a *Shaft*. Details are added using both the *Shaft* and *Groove* commands.

Section 1: Creating Shafts.

1) Start a **New 3D part** and name it ***T33Shaft***, make your **PartBody** the **In Work Object** and, enter the **Sketcher** on the **yz plane**.

2) Set your length units to be inches (**Tools** – **Options... – Parameters and Measures**)

3) Draw and **Constrain** the following **Profile** and **Axis**.

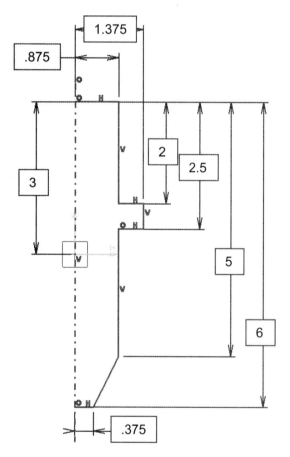

4) **Exit** the Sketcher and **Shaft** the sketch through an angle of **360deg** using the **Sketch Axis** as the Axis Selection.

5) Enter the **Sketcher** on the **zx plane**.

6) Use the **Project 3D Silhouette Edges** to project all the edges of the part as **Construction Elements**.

7) Draw an **Axis** that is on and parallel to the V axis.

8) Using the projections as a guide, draw a **Profile** around the outline of the part on the right side of the axis as a **Standard Element**.

9) Offset the profile to the outside of the part. Select all elements of the profile you created in the previous step. Select the **Offset** icon. Activate the `Offset:` field in the *Value field* using the **TAB** key. Enter *0.5* and hit the **TAB** key again.

10) Turn the original profile into a **Construction Element**.

11) **Exit** the Sketcher.

12) Select the **Shaft** icon. In the *Shaft Definition* window, set the `First angle:` to be *180deg*, **Reverse Direction** and use the **Sketch Axis** as the `Axis Selection:`. Select the **More>>** button, activate the `Thick Profile` toggle and set `Thickness1:` to be *.125 in*.

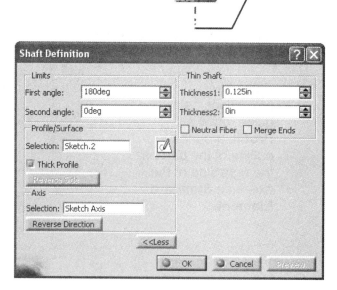

13) Enter the **Sketcher** on the **zx plane** and draw and **Constrain** the **Rectangle** shown.

14) **Exit** the *Sketcher* and **Shaft** the sketch *180deg* using the Z-axis as the rotation axis. (Note: You may have to *Reverse Direction* to get the desired effect.)

Center axis

15) **Propagate**.

Section 2: Creating Grooves.

1) Enter the **Sketcher** on the **zx plane**.

2) Draw and **Constrain** the following **Profile**.

3) **Exit** the Sketcher.

4) Select the **Groove** icon. In the *Groove Definition* window, set the First angle: to be **360deg** and use the Z-axis as the rotation axis. Select the **More>>** button, activate the Thick Profile toggle and set Thickness1: to be **0.03 in**. Select **OK**.

5) Double click on **Groove.1** in the specification tree.

6) In the Groove Definition window, set Thickness2: to be **0.03 in**.

7) Enter the **Sketcher** on the **zx plane**. Draw and **Constrain** the **Circle** shown.

8) **Exit** the *Sketcher* and create a ***360 deg*** **Groove** using the sketch.

9) Edit **Shaft.3**. In the Shaft Definition window set the rotation angle to be ***360deg***.

10) Enter the **Sketcher** on the **yz plane**.

11) Draw and **Constrain** the **Circle** shown. The center of the circle lies on the center axis.

D.125

.163

12) **Exit** the *Sketcher* and

Pad the circle **2** inches in both directions (Mirrored extent).

13) **Propagate**.

NOTES:

Chapter 3:
PART DESIGN

Tutorial 3.4: Sketch-Based Features: Advanced commands

FEATURED TOPICS & COMMANDS

MULTI-SECTION SOLID 2

RIBS AND SLOTS 2

STIFFENERS 2

TUTORIAL 3.4 START 3

    Section 1: Multi-sections Solid 3

    Section 2: Creating Ribs and Slots 11

    Section 3: Creating Stiffeners 17

PREREQUISITE KNOWLEDGE & COMMANDS

- The *Sketcher* workbench and associated commands
- Editing a preexisting sketch
- Pads
- Rotating the part using the mouse or compass

MULTI-SECTION SOLID

A *Multi-sections Solid* is generated by two or more planar sections that are swept along a spine. A *Multi-sections Solid* can add material or remove material. The planar sections may also be connected with guidelines which act as boundaries in which the *Multi-sections Solid* is contained. Direction arrows show the orientation of the *Multi-sections Solid* and can be used to change the orientation. *Multi-sections Solids* are very useful in creating transitions between two existing solids.

Note: It seems that, starting with V5R17, the spine curve must be created before the Multi-sections Solid. Otherwise CATIA will not allow you re-enter the *Multi-sections Solid* definition window and select the curve.

RIBS AND SLOTS

A *Rib* is a profile swept along a center curve (open or closed) to create a solid feature. *Ribs* are useful when you need to sweep a profile from one surface to another. A *Rib* may also be used to create a pipe like feature by sweeping a profile along a center curve.

A *Slot* is a profile swept along a center curve (open or closed) to remove material from a solid.

The center curve used to create *Ribs* and *Slots* do not have to be drawn to the feature's true length. Walls of existing parts may be used as boundaries.

STIFFENERS

A *Stiffener* is a brace that is added to a wall or other structures that need to be strengthened to prevent possible breakage. It is often used in castings and molded plastics.

TUTORIAL 3.4 START

The part created in this tutorial is a representation of a boat. Notice the sloping surface of the boats hull (Multi-sections Solid), the thin support members (stiffeners), and the ribs and slots that are part of the outer shell.

Section 1: Multi-sections Solid

1.1 – Creating a Simple Loft

1) Start a **New 3D Part** name it *T34Boat* and, make your **PartBody** the **In Work Object**, change your **units** to **Millimeters**, and enter the **Sketcher** on the **zx plane**.

2) Draw and **Constrain** the following **Ellipse**. The ellipse's center coincides with the origin and the axes are along the V and H coordinate directions. (Hint: To constrain the ellipse, select the ellipse in the approximate location of the dimension and then select the origin.)

3) Draw a **Line** that cuts the ellipse in half as shown.

4) **Quick Trim** the top portion of the ellipse.

5) **Exit** the Sketcher and deselect all.

6) Create a new **Plane** by offsetting the **zx-plane** by *50 mm*. In the *Plane Definition* window, activate the **Repeat object after OK** toggle. After you select **OK** an *Object Repetition* window will appear. Enter *4* instances.

7) Create the same number of new planes on the other side of the sketch as shown.

Enter the Sketcher on this plane.

Center point

8) Enter the **Sketcher** on the first new plane to the right of the sketch (Plane.1 in your tree). See above figure.

9) Project Sketch.1 onto the new plane using **3D Project Elements**. To select the entire sketch all at once, select Sketch.1 in the specification tree.

10) Scale the projection by 80% using the following procedure. Select all elements of the projection and then select the **Scale** icon. Select the scaling center point as shown in the figure, activate the **Duplicate mode**, and enter *0.8* in the Value: field.

11) Turn the original projection into a **Construction Element**.

12) **Exit** the *Sketcher*.

13) Repeat the above procedure to create 4 more sketches all scaled 80% from that of the previously sketch.

14) Repeat for the other side using the scale method, or **3D Project Element** the scaled sketches on the right side onto the plane on the left side.

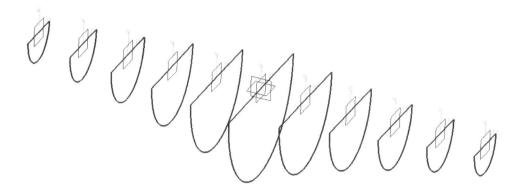

15) **Propagate**

16) Create a Multi-sections Solid using the 6 sketches on the right. Deselect all elements.

Select the **Multi-sections Solid** icon. Select the middle (biggest) sketch and then each sketch in order from left to right. After you have selected the last sketch on the right, select **OK**.

17) Repeat for the other side. However, the largest sketch now must be selected in the specification tree (this is because it is already part of a solid). The largest sketch which should be **Sketch.1**. The other sketches may still be selected manually with the mouse.

18) Locate the *Dress-Up Features* toolbar .

19) **Shell** the solid to a thickness of **5 mm** removing the top face.

Face to remove

Shell Definition

Default inside thickness:	5mm
Default outside thickness:	0mm
Faces to remove:	Multi-sections Solid.2\Fa
Other thickness faces:	No selection

☐ Propagate faces to remove

More>>

OK   Cancel

20) **Edge Fillet** the inside and outside joint between the 2 halves of the boat with a radius of **20 mm**.

21) **Propagate**

1.2 – Relimiting a Multi-sections Solid

By default a Multi-sections Solid will begin and end with the planar section chosen. However, if you use guidelines or a spline to direct your Multi-sections Solid, you can relimit it to begin or end with these curves.

1) Offset a **Plane**

 from the right end of the boat by **30 mm**.

2) Enter the **Sketcher** on the newly offset plane.

3) **3D Project Elements** the end of the boat onto the sketch plane as a **Standard Element** and then **Scale** the projection by a value of *0.1* using the same procedure as before. Turn the original projection into a **Construction Element**.

4) **Exit** the *Sketcher* and re-enter the **Sketcher** on the **yz-plane**.

5) **3D Project Elements** the end of the boat onto the sketch plane as a **Construction Element**.

6) Draw and **Constrain** the **Spline** shown.

7) **Exit** the *Sketcher*, deselect all, and **Multi-sections Solid** 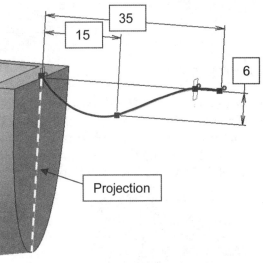 the end of the boat with the scaled version of the boat end. Select the sketch used to create the end of the boat. This will be located in **Multi-sections Solid.1** the last sketch (**Sketch.6**) and then the small scaled sketch.

(Having Trouble? If the loft looks funny, like shown below, edit *Multi-sections Solid.3* and change the direction of *Close point 2* by clicking on the arrow.)

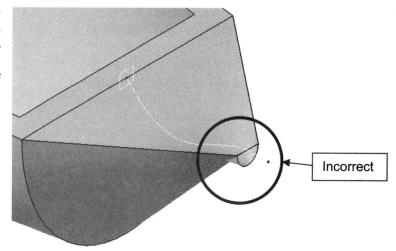

Incorrect

8) **Propagate**

9) Double click on **Multi-sections Solid.3**. In the *Multi-sections Solid Definition* window, select the **Spine** tab. Activate the Spine: field and select the spline. Select **OK**. Notice the difference.

Spline

10) Double click on **Multi-sections Solid.3**. In the *Multi-sections Solid Definition* window, select the **Relimitation** tab and deselect the **Relimited on end section** toggle. Select **OK**. Notice the difference.

11) Double click on **Multi-sections Solid.3**. *Remove* the spline and reactivate the *Relimited on end section* toggle.

Section 2: Creating Ribs and Slots

2.1 – Creating a Simple Slot

1) Enter the **Sketcher** on the **xy-plane**.

2) **3D Project Elements** the outer profile of the boat onto the sketch plane. (The projection in the figure is shown black, however the real projection will be yellow.)

3) **Exit** the *Sketcher* and re-enter the **Sketcher** on the **zx-plane**.

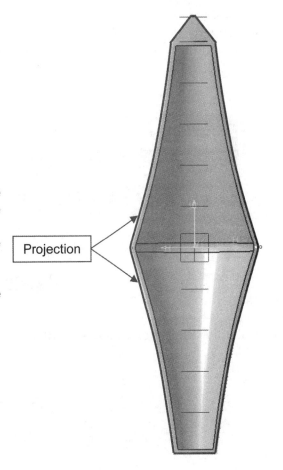

Projection

4) Draw and **Constrain** the following **Profile**. Use **Cut Part By Sketch Plane** to get a better view.

5) **Exit** the Sketcher and create a slot that goes around the boat using the above sketch and the projection. Select the **Slot** icon. The Profile is the sketch created in step 4, and the Center curve is the projection created in step 3. If a *Warning* window appears, **Close** it.

6) Enter the **Sketcher** on the **xy-plane**.

7) Draw and **Constrain** the *5 mm* diameter **Circle** as shown.

8) **Exit** the *Sketcher* and re-enter the **Sketcher** on the plane indicated in the figure. (The first offset plane created in this tutorial.)

Enter the *Sketcher* on this plane

9) **3D Project Elements** Sketch.2 (the sketch used to create this section of the boat) onto the sketch plane. Use **Cut Part By Sketch Plane** to get a better look.

10) Isolate the projection and delete the top line of the sketch. (**Insert** – **Operation** – **3D Geometry** – **Isolate**.)

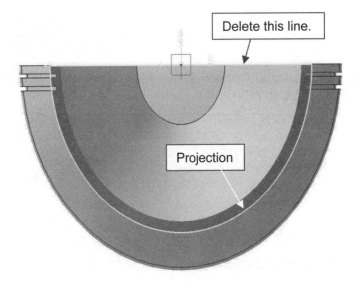

Delete this line.

Projection

11) **Exit** the *Sketcher* and create a rib using the above circle and projection. Select the **Rib** icon. Use the circle as the `Profile` and the projection as the `Center curve`.

12) Create a similar **Rib** on the other side as shown in the figure. This time you will project Sketch.7.

13) **Propagate**.

14) Enter the **Sketcher** on the top surface of the boat as shown in the figure.

Enter Sketcher on this surface

15) Draw and **Constrain** the *4 mm* diameter **Circle** shown.

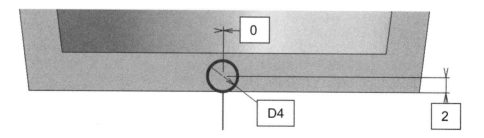

16) **Exit** the Sketcher and re-enter the **Sketcher** on the **yz-plane**.

17) **3D Project Elements** the top edge of the left end of the boat on to the sketch plane as a **Construction Element**. The projection will appear as a point.

Project this line

Projection point

18) Draw and **Constrain** the following **Profile**. Notice that the bottom of the profile is **Coincident** with the projection point and the top vertical line is **Tangent** with the radius.

19) **Exit** the *Sketcher* and create a **Rib** using the circle as the Profile and the vertical sketch as the Center curve.

Rib Definition

Profile   Sketch.20
Center curve Sketch.21
Profile control
Keep angle
Selection: No selection
☐ Move profile to path
☐ Merge rib's ends ☐ Thick Profile
Thin Rib
Thickness1: 1mm
Thickness2: 0mm
☐ Neutral Fiber ☐ Merge Ends
[OK] [Cancel] [Preview]

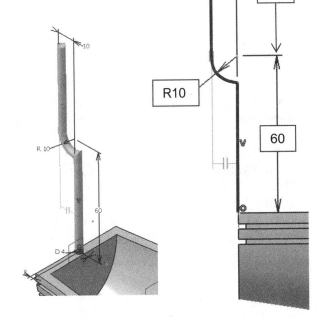

10

50

R10

60

20) Enter the **Sketcher** on the **yz-plane**.

21) Draw and **Constrain** the following **Rectangle**.

22) **Exit** the *Sketcher* and **Pad** the rectangle to a length of *3 mm* and **Mirror extents**.

23) Enter the **Sketcher** on the top of the rectangle (flag) and draw a circle as shown in the figure. Approximate the size.

24) **Exit** the Sketcher and re-enter the **Sketcher** on the front face of the flag. **3D Project Elements** the front face of the flag onto the sketch plane as a **Construction Element**. Draw a **Spline** that starts and ends at the top of the flag like that shown in the figure. (Do not make it too complex or you may get an error when trying to apply the *Slot*.)

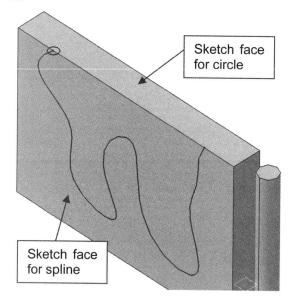

Sketch face for circle

Sketch face for spline

25) **Exit** the Sketcher and create a **Slot** using the circle as the Profile and the spline as the Center curve.

26) Create a **Slot** using the circle as the Profile and the spline as the Center curve. Activate the **Merge slot's ends** toggle. If a *Warning* window appears, **Close** it.

Slot Definition	
Profile	Sketch.23
Center curve	Sketch.24

Profile control

Keep angle ▼

Selection: No selection

☐ Move profile to path

☑ Merge slot's ends ☐ Thick Profile

Thin Slot

Thickness1: 1mm

Thickness2: 0mm

☐ Neutral Fiber ☐ Merge Ends

[OK] [Cancel] [Preview]

27) **Propagate**.

Section 3: Creating Stiffeners

1) Enter the **Sketcher** on the **xy-plane**.

2) **3D Project Elements** the left and right inner profiles of the boat on to the sketch plane as **Construction Elements**.

3) Draw and **Constrain** the **Line** shown in the figure.

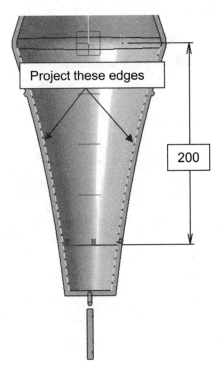

Project these edges

200

4) **Exit** the *Sketcher* and create a stiffener that travels from the top down using the following procedure. Deselect all. Select the **Stiffener** icon. Activate the **From Top** toggle. Set Thickness1 to *2 mm*. Activate the Selection: field and select the line.

5) Enter the **Sketcher** on the **xy-plane**.

6) **3D Project Elements** the inner outline of the boat behind the stiffener as a **Construction Element**.

7) Draw the **Lines** shown.

8) **Exit** the *Sketcher* and create a *2 mm* thick **Stiffener** that travels **from** the **top** down using the crossed lines as the profile.

9) On your own, draw and **Pad** a seat in the boat and support the seat with a **Stiffener** as shown.

10) **Propagate**.

NOTES:

Chapter 3: PART DESIGN

Tutorial 3.5: Dress-Up Features: Drafts, Fillets & Chamfers

FEATURED TOPICS & COMMANDS

THE DRESS-UP FEATURES TOOLBAR 2

THE DRAFTS TOOLBAR 2

THE FILLETS TOOLBAR 3

TUTORIAL 3.5 START 3

    Section 1: Creating Drafts 3

    Section 2: Creating Fillets...9

    Section 3: Creating Chamfers 18

PREREQUISITE KNOWLEDGE & COMMANDS

- The *Sketcher* workbench and associated commands
- Editing a preexisting sketch
- Pads and Pockets
- Rotating the part using the mouse or compass

THE DRESS-UP FEATURES TOOLBAR

Dress-up features allow you to add finishing touches to your part. These commands are not based on a sketch. All parameters of the feature are controlled from the *Definition* window. The commands included in the *Dress-up Features* toolbar are

- The Fillets toolbar: The commands contained in the *Fillets* toolbar put radii on sharp corners. Several options are available.
- Chamfer: A *Chamfer* is a bevel created between 2 surfaces.
- The Drafts toolbar: The *Drafts* toolbar contains commands that will place an angle on a surface. Several options are available.
- Shell: The *Shell* command takes a solid part and hollows it out while keeping a given thickness on its sides.
- Thickness: The *Thickness* command adds material uniformly to a surface.
- Thread: Allows you to create threads or taps. The helix thread form is not shown in 3D; however, the information is stored and will show on a 2D drawing.
- The Remove Face toolbar: Allows you to remove or replace a face.

THE DRAFTS TOOLBAR

A *Draft* is an angled face. Material gets added or removed from your part when a draft is applied. The amount of material added and/or removed depends on the draft angle and the location of the neutral surface. Reading from left to right, the commands in the *Drafts* toolbar are

- Draft Angle: Applies a simple draft angle to a surface.
- Draft Reflect Line: This command allows you to draft from a line to a limiting element. It is a complex command and needs to be experimented with to understand its complete usefulness.
- Variable Angle Draft: This command allows you to specify different draft angles to a surface.

When applying a draft, you should keep in mind the following basic draft definitions.

- Pull direction: This is the direction that the draft angle is measured from.
- Draft angle: This is the angle that the draft faces make with the pulling direction.
- Neutral element: This is the element that remains unchanged after the draft command is applied.
- Parting element: This element defines where the draft is to start.
- Limiting elements: Define a region in which the draft should be applied.
- Points: This is used to define the locations where the draft angle varies when using a variable draft.

(Note: A draft angle can never be negative.)

THE FILLETS TOOLBAR

A *Fillet* is a rounded edge or corner of constant or variable radius that is tangent to the two surfaces that create the edge. Reading from left to right, the commands in the *Fillets* toolbar are

- Edge fillet: This command creates a smooth transition between two surfaces.
- Variable radius fillet: This command allows the fillet to have more than one radius.
- Chordal fillet: This command allows you to control the width of the fillet (distance between the 2 rolling edges) which is also called as chordal length.
- Face-face fillet: This command is used when there is no intersection between the two surfaces or when there are more than two sharp edges between the surfaces.
- Tritangent fillet: This command involves removing one of the 3 surfaces selected.

TUTORIAL 3.5 START

The part created in this tutorial is shown at two different stages of the process. Notice the angled surfaces (drafts), the rounded corners (fillets) and the beveled edges (chamfers).

Section 1: Creating Drafts

1.1 - Creating Simple Drafts

1) Start a **New 3D Part** name it *T35AngledBase* and, make your **PartBody** the **In Work Object**, change your **units** to **Millimeters**, and enter the **Sketcher** on the **yz plane**.

2) Draw and **Constrain** the following **Profile**.

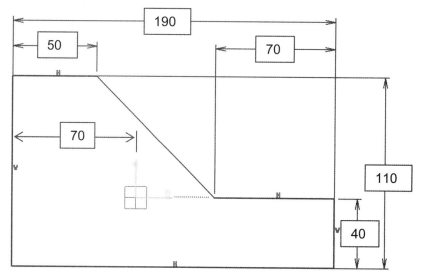

1) **Exit** the *Sketcher* and **Pad** the sketch to a length of **100 mm**.

2) Apply a constant **20° Draft Angle** to the right face of the part using the top face as the neutral element. The pulling direction should point up.

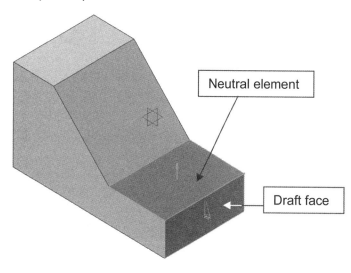

Neutral element

Draft face

3) Apply a constant *15° Draft Angle* to the front, back and left side faces of the part using all of the top faces as the neutral elements. The pulling direction should point up.

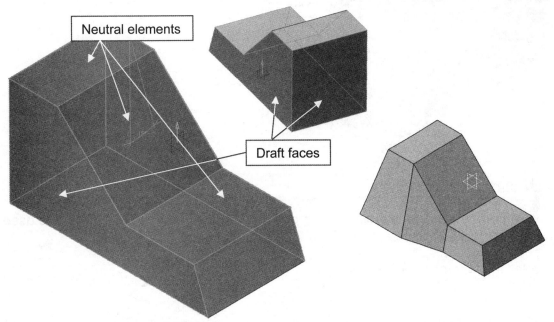

Neutral elements

Draft faces

4) Edit **Draft.2** (the draft applied to the 3 sides) by double clicking on it in the specification tree and change the neutral faces from the 3 top surfaces to just the lowest one. Activate the *Neutral Element Selection* and click on the very top surface and the angled surface to deselect them.

(Notice: The neutral face indicated in the figure is the only face that remains unchanged.)

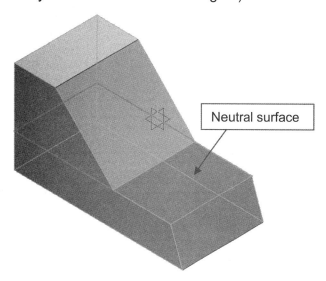

Neutral surface

1.2 - Using a Parting Element:

A *parting element* is a plane, face or surface that cuts the part in two. It is used as a boundary to tell the computer where to stop or change the draft angle.

1) Enter the **Sketcher** on the top face of the part.

2) Use **3D Project Element** to project the top face rectangle onto the sketch plane as a **Standard Element**.

Sketch face

Projected face

3) **Exit** the *Sketcher* and **Pad** the projection to a length of *60 mm*.

4) Create a **Plane** that is offset *-20 mm* from the top surface of the part.

Offset this surface

5) Create a *10° Draft Angle* using the offset plane as a parting element. Select the 4 sides of the *Pad* as the Face(s) to draft and the offset plane as the Neutral Element. Select the **More>>** icon and activate the **Parting = Neutral** toggle. The pulling direction should point up. (Note: A curved surface may also be used as a parting element.)

4 Draft faces

Neutral Element

1.3 - Trimming Draft Features

1) Edit **Draft.1** (The first draft created on the end of the part.) by double clicking on it.

2) Select the **More>>** icon in the *Draft Definition* window. Activate the `Limiting Element(s):` right click and select **Create Plane**. Create a plane that is offset **30 mm** from the **yz plane**. Repeat and create a plane that is offset **70 mm** from the **yz plane**. Click on the Orange arrows attached to the offset plane to change their direction to point inward towards each other and apply the draft.

3) Reenter the Draft Definition window and change the direction of the Orange arrows to the outward position and apply the draft and notice the difference.

1.4 - Variable Drafts:

A *Variable Angle Draft* allows you to change the draft angle along the surface.

1) **Propagate**.

2) Enter the **Sketcher** on the top of the base.

3) Draw and **Constrain** the **Rectangle** as shown. The rectangle is drawn *10 mm* away from all sides.

4) **Exit** the *Sketcher* and **Pocket** the sketch using the **Up to Last** option.

5) Create a 40/10 degree **Variable Angle Draft** on the inside left face of the pocket using the top face as the Neutral Element. Once you pick a neutral element, the computer automatically selects 2 points.

Add 2 more points by creating 2 planes that are offset from the **yz plane** by *30* and *70 mm*. Double click on the dimensions to change their values.

Section 2: Creating Fillets

2.1 - Creating Simple Fillets

1) **Propagate**.

2) Create a **5 mm** radius **Edge Fillet** on the top right side edge between the two drafted surfaces.

Filleted edge

3) Create a **5 mm** radius **Edge Fillet** around the very top face of the part.

Filleted face

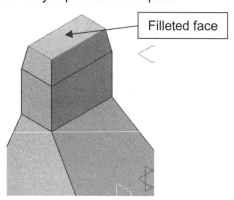

Sketch face

4) Enter the **Sketcher** on the very top surface of the part.

5) Draw and **Constrain** the **10 mm** diameter **Circle** shown. The circle is in the middle of the top surface.

(**Problems?** If your circle does not fit, go back and edit *Draft.2* and make sure that you have selected the proper neutral surface.)

23.5

D10

8

6) **Exit** the *Sketcher* and **Pad** the circle to a length of **40 mm**.

7) Create a **5 mm Edge Fillet** around the bottom edge of the pin.

Filleted edge

2.2 - Rolling on an Edge:

The *Rolling on an Edge* option allows you to create a fillet that has a larger radius than the distance of the sides supporting the fillet.

1) **Propagate**.

2) Enter the **Sketcher** on the right face of the object between the drafted surfaces.

Sketch face

3) **3D Project Elements** the sketch face as a **Construction Element**.

4) Draw and **Constrain** the **Rectangle** as shown. Picking the top and bottom lines of the rectangle to create the 20 mm constraint will make it less likely that the rectangle will move out of position.

20

5) **Exit** the *Sketcher* and **Pad** the rectangle to a length of **40 mm**.

6) Enter the **Sketcher** on the same face as before.

7) **3D Project Elements** the sketch face as a **Construction Element**.

8) Draw and **Constrain** the **Rectangle** as shown.

9) **Exit** the *Sketcher* and **Pad** the rectangle to a length of **10 mm**.

10) Try to apply a **40 mm** radius **Edge Fillet** to the step. You will get an error because the step height is less than 40 mm. Select **OK** in the *Update Error* window. Select **Yes** in the *Feature Definition Error* window. When the *Edge Fillet Definition* window reappears, activate the Edge(s) to Keep: field and select the top edge of the step.

Filleted edge

Edge to keep

Filleted Edge

11) **Propagate**.

12) Enter the **Sketcher** on the **yz-plane**.

13) Draw and **Constrain** the **Rectangle** as shown. The reason that there are to vertical 30 mm constraints is that one constrains the height of the rectangle and one constrains the rectangle to the object.

14) **Exit** the Sketcher and **Pad** the rectangle using 2 limits. The first limit has a length of **120 mm** and the second has a length of **20 mm**.

15) Apply a **10 mm** Edge Fillet 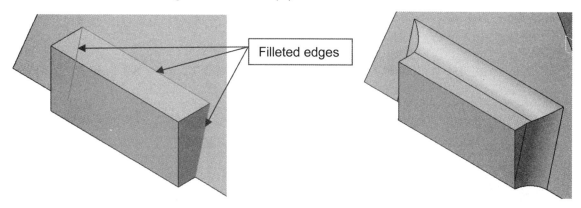 to the edges shown. (Notice that the edges between the filleted edges remain sharp.)

Filleted edges

16) Reenter the *Edge Fillet Definition* window by double clicking on **EdgeFillet.5**. Select the **More>>** button. Keep the 2 edges indicated. (Notice that the edges are rounded now.) Repeat for the other side.

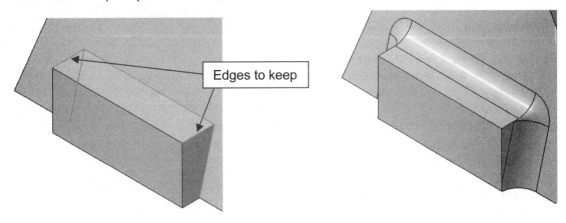

Edges to keep

2.3 - Limiting Fillets:

Limiting a fillet allows you to apply a fillet to only a portion of an edge.

1) **Propagate**.

2) Apply a *10 mm* radius **Edge Fillet** to the top portion of the angled edges of the part using the **zx-plane** as a Limiting Element. Click on the orange arrow to change direction of fillet travel if necessary.

Angled edges

2.4 - Face to Face Fillets:

A *Face to Face Fillet* allows you to create a fillet between two surfaces that do not touch.

1) **Propagate**.

2) Delete **Draft.4** and **Pocket.1** by right clicking on them in the specification tree and selecting **Delete**.

(**Having Trouble?** If deleting the draft or pocket causes your part to turn red, fill in the area drawing a Rectangle and Padding it 40 mm.)

3) Enter the **Sketcher** on the top face of the base.

4) Draw and **Constrain** the **30 mm** diameter **Circles** shown.

5) **Exit** the *Sketcher* and **Pad** the circles to a length of **20 mm**.

Sketch face

Face/Pad.1/PartBody

6) Put a **30° Draft Angle** on the surfaces of the cylinders.

Draft faces

Neutral Element

7) Create a **15 mm Face To Face Fillet** between the two cones. This is a complex operation. If error windows appear, close them.

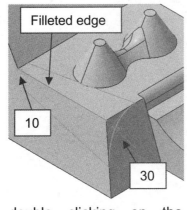

2.5 - Variable Fillets:

Variable Fillets enable you to produce a fillet with a variable radius.

1) **Propagate**.

2) Create a **Variable Fillet** on the edge indicated that starts off at a **10 mm** radius and ends up at a **30 mm** radius using a **Linear** variation. Change the fillet radii by double clicking on the dimensions.

Filleted edge

10

30

3) Repeat the **Edge Fillet** on the other side using the **Cubic** Variation.

(Note: There are Drafted filleted pads and pockets available that do both commands simultaneously.)

<u>Section 3:</u> Creating Chamfers

1) Create a **3 mm** x **45°** **Chamfer** on the right face of the projection shown.

2) **Propagate**.

Chapter 3:
PART DESIGN

Tutorial 3.6: Dress-Up Features: Shell, Thickness & Threads

FEATURED TOPICS & COMMANDS

SHELLS 2

THICKNESS 2

THREADS AND TAPS 2

TUTORIAL 3.6 START 3

    Section 1: Applying a Shell. 4

    Section 2: Adding Thickness 8

    Section 3: Creating Threads 9

PREREQUISITE KNOWLEDGE & COMMANDS

- The *Sketcher* workbench and associated commands
- Editing a preexisting sketch
- Pads, Pockets, Shafts and Holes
- Fillets and Drafts
- Rotating the part using the mouse or compass

SHELLS

The *Shell* command is part of the *Dress-Up Features* toolbar. Shelling consists of emptying a part out while keeping a given thickness on its sides. One or more faces may be selected to be open and the remaining sides can have different thicknesses.

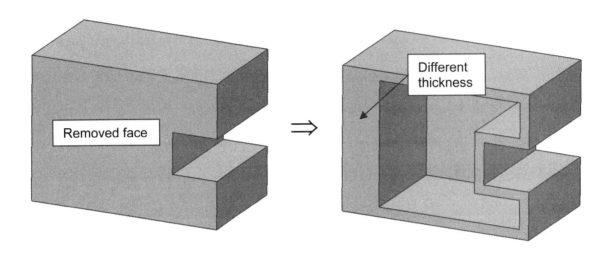

THICKNESS

The *Thickness* command is part of the *Dress-Up Features* toolbar. This command allows you to add thickness to a wall.

THREADS AND TAPS

The *Thread* command is part of the *Dress-Up Features* toolbar. The *Thread* command allows you to create threads in accordance to drawing standards. User specified threads may also be implemented. The threads cannot be viewed in the 3D space. However, they will appear on the orthographic projection of the part that is created in the *Drafting* workbench.

In the *Part Design* workbench, there is a command called *Tap – Thread Analysis*. It is located in the *Analysis* toolbar. This command calls out all threads on the part. However, the call out that CATIA gives is not in accordance with ASME thread note standards.

TUTORIAL 3.6 START

Three different views of the part modeled in this tutorial are shown below. The part is shown as a cut away view to show the inner features. The main solid is created using the *Shaft* command and is hollowed out using the *Shell* command. *Drafts, Fillets, Threads, Thickness* and *Holes* are added to finish the part. Notice that the threads cannot be seen in the 3D view, but are represented on the section view created in the *Drafting* workbench.

Thread symbol

Section view A-A
Scale: 1:1

Section 1: Applying a Shell.

1) Start a **New 3D Part** name it ***T36ThreadedSupport*** and, make your **PartBody** the **In Work Object**, change your **units** to **inches**, and

   enter the **Sketcher** 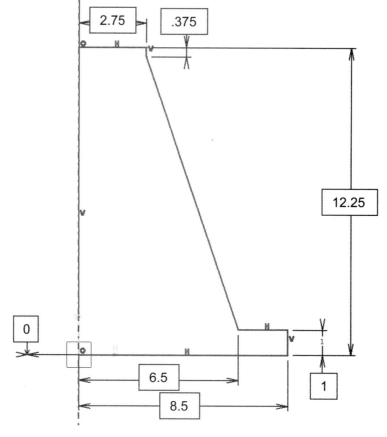 on the **yz plane**.

2) Draw and **Constrain** the following **Axis** and **Profile**.

3) **Exit** the *Sketcher* and **Shaft** the sketch ***360 deg*** using the Sketch Axis as the Axis.

4) Pull out the *Dress-Up Features* toolbar

5) **Shell** the part using a uniform thickness of *.625 in* and removing the bottom face of the part.

Shell Definition	
Default inside thickness:	0.625in
Default outside thickness:	0in
Faces to remove:	Shaft.1\Face.1
Other thickness faces:	No selection
☑ Propagate faces to remove	

More>>

OK   Cancel

Remove this face.

6) **Edge Fillet** the edges indicated in the figure with a *0.25 in* radius. 5 edges in total.

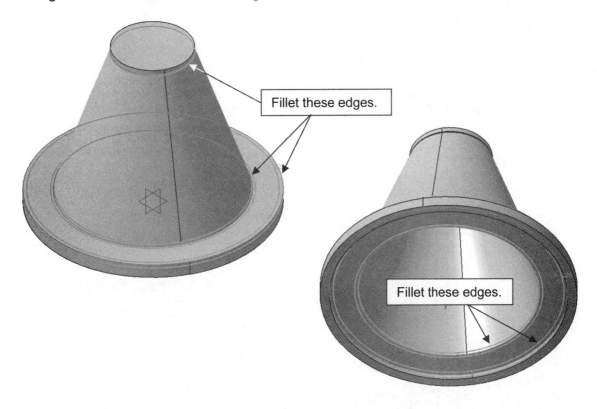

Fillet these edges.

Fillet these edges.

7) Enter the **Sketcher** on the top face of the part.

8) Draw and **Constrain** the **Circle** shown. The circle's center coincides with the origin.

Sketch face

D4.75

9) **Exit** the *Sketcher* and **Pad** the sketch through the part *9 in*.

10) Change your view mode to **Wireframe** . This icon is located in the *View* toolbar located in the bottom toolbar area.

11) **Propagate**.

12) Put a **Draft Angle** of *2 deg* on the padded cylinder that travels through your part using the top surface of the part as the Neutral Element. You may have to reverse the orange arrow so that the cylinder becomes smaller as it travels down.

13) Change your view mode back to **Shading with Edges** .

14) Enter the **Sketcher** on the top face of the part.

15) Draw and **Constrain** the **Circle** shown. The circle's center coincides with the origin.

16) **Exit** the *Sketcher* and **Pocket** the sketch using the **Up to last** option.

17) **Edge Fillet** the edge indicated in the figure with a *0.5 in* radius.

Filleted edge

Section 2: Adding Thickness

1) Add 0.5 in of thickness to the top face of the part. Select the **Thickness** icon. Activate the Default thickness faces: field and select the top face of the part. Enter a thickness of *0.5 in* in the Default thickness: field.

Add thickness to this face.

Thickness Definition

Default thickness: 0.5in

Default thickness faces : 1 Face

Other thickness faces : No selection

OK Cancel

Section 3: Creating Threads

1) **Propagate**.

2) Apply a thread to the hole running down through the part.   Select the **Thread** icon. Fill in the following fields;

- Lateral Face: Select the circumferential surface of the hole
- Limit Face: Select the top surface of the part
- Type: **No Standard**
- Thread Diameter: *2 in*
- Thread Depth: *9.5 in*
- Pitch: *.222 in*
- Activate the **Right-Threaded** toggle.
- Notice that even though you cannot see the threads, the specification tree contains the thread information.

Limit face

Lateral face

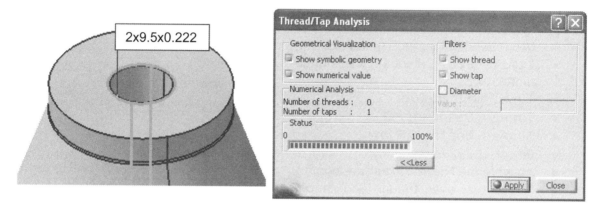

3) Select the **Thread – Tap Analysis** icon in the *Analysis* toolbar. In the *Thread/Tap Analysis* window select the **More>>** button to see all the available options and then select **Apply**. Notice that a call out appears on the thread giving the thread information. Note that a more conventional thread call out for this particular thread would be **2 – 4.5 UNC – ⩡9.5** where 4.5 is one over the pitch.

4) Create a Counterbored **Hole** in the bottom lip of the part with the following parameters;
   - Counterbore diameter: *1 in*
   - Counterbore depth: *0.125 in*
   - Hole diameter: *0.625 in*.

5) Create 3 more counter bored holes using a *Circular Pattern*. Select the **Circular Pattern** icon located in the *Transformation Features* toolbar. In the *Circular Pattern Definition* window, fill in the following fields;

- Object: Click on the counterbored hole
- Parameters: **Instance(s) & angular spacing**
- Instance(s): *4*
- Angular spacing: *90 deg*
- Reference element: select the circumferential surface of the base

Reference element

6) **Propagate**.

NOTES:

Chapter 3: PART DESIGN

Tutorial 3.7: Transformation Features

FEATURED TOPICS & COMMANDS

THE TRANSFORATION FEATURES TOOLBAR...2

THE TRANSFORMATIONS TOOLBAR...2

THE PATTERNS TOOLBAR..3

TUTORIAL 3.7 START..3

Section 1: Creating circular patterns. 4

Section 2: Mirroring a part. 7

Section 3: Creating rectangular patterns. 12

Section 4: Transformations..13

PREREQUISITE KNOWLEDGE & COMMANDS

- The *Sketcher* workbench and associated commands
- Editing a preexisting sketch
- Pads and Pockets
- Rotating the part using the mouse or compass

THE TRANSFORATION FEATURES TOOLBAR

The *Transformation Features* toolbar contains commands that transform, move or create a pattern or array of a feature. Reading from left to right, the commands located in the *Transformation Features* toolbar are

- The Transformation toolbar: The *Transformation* toolbar contains commands that allow you to move, rotate and create a mirror image of a part.
- Mirror: The *Mirror* command creates a duplicate mirror image of a part.

- The Patterns toolbar: The *Pattern* toolbar allows you to create arrays of an existing feature.
- The Scale toolbar: The *Scale* toolbar contains commands that may be used to scale a part. The *Scale* command changes the size of a part relative to a selected plane or point. Scaling can only occur in one direction at a time. The *Affinity* command transforms the absolute size by multiplying a scale ratio.

THE TRANSFORMATIONS TOOLBAR

A transformation is the ability to move a body either by translating it along an axis, rotating it around an axis or moving it symmetrically about a plane. A body cannot be duplicated during transformation. Reading from left to right, the commands located in the *Transformation* toolbar are

- Translation: *Translation* moves the part in a selected linear direction.
- Rotation: *Rotation* rotates a part around a selected line or axis.
- Symmetry: *Symmetry* replaces the part with its mirror image.
- AxisToAxis: *AxisToAxis* transform a geometry's position relative to one axis system into a new axis system.

When transforming a part, CATIA will prompt you with a *Question* window to make sure it is okay to violate the constraints that were imposed in the *Sketcher*. If you are sure you want to continue with the transformation, click <u>Y</u>es.

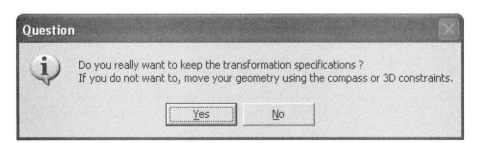

THE PATTERNS TOOLBAR

Patterns allow you to create arrays of an existing feature. You can create rectangular or polar arrays. The positions of the feature may also be manually defined. Patterned features are connected or associative. Therefore, if the original feature is changed all the patterned features will change. You can break the connection between the features by exploding the pattern. To explode the pattern, right click on the pattern feature in the specification tree and select *Pattern object - Explode...* Reading from left to right, the commands located in the *Patterns* toolbar are

- Rectangular Pattern: This command enables you to create rectangular arrays of a feature with a specified number of rows and columns.
- Circular Pattern: This command enables you to create polar arrays of a feature.
- User Pattern: This command allows you to create several instances of a feature in predefined locations. The locations are defined by the user in a sketch which usually consists of several points.

TUTORIAL 3.7 START

The part modeled in this tutorial is a simplified representation of a bicycle chain ring. It contains some features that do not exist on a chain ring, but are created to illustrate a particular command. Ignoring the rectangular holes in the right arm, notice the parts symmetry and repeated features.

Section 1: Creating circular patterns.

1) Start a **New 3D Part** name it **T37Sprocket** and, make your **PartBody** the **In Work Object**, change your **units** to **inches**, and enter the **Sketcher** 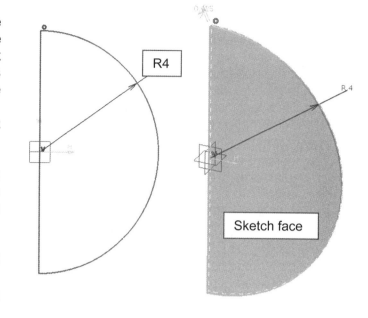 on the **yz plane**.

2) Draw and constrain the following sketch. Notice that the center of the arc is coincident with the origin.

3) **Exit** the Sketcher and **Pad** the sketch to a length of **0.125 in**.

4) Enter the **Sketcher** on the front face of the Sprocket.

5) Draw and constrain the **Construction Element** sketch shown.

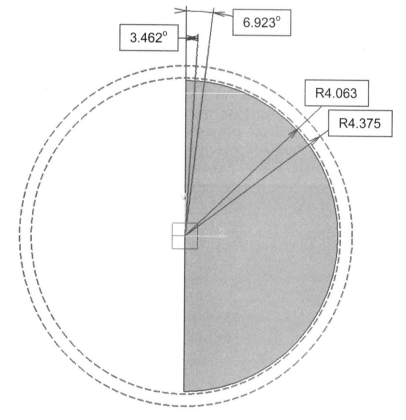

6) **3D Project Elements** the face of the part on to the sketch plane as a **Construction Element**.

7) Using the construction lines as a guide, draw and constrain the sketch shown. The sides of the tooth are constructed using the **Profile** command and the *Tangent arc* option. The top of the tooth is created using the *Three Point Arc* option.

8) **Exit** the Sketcher and **Pad** the sketch to a length of *.125 in*. Reverse the direction if necessary.

9) Pull out the *Transformation Features* toolbar .

10) **Propagate**.

11) Create a circular pattern of the chain ring tooth. Select the **Circular Pattern** icon. In the *Circular Pattern Definition* window, fill in the following fields;

- Parameters: **Instance(s) & angular spacing**
- Instance(s): *26*
- Angular spacing: *6.923deg*
- Reference element: Select the top of the tooth (You may have to zoom in to do this.)
- Object: select **Pad.2** (the pad used to create the tooth) in the specification tree. Reverse the direction if necessary.

Reference element for pattern.

Section 2: Mirroring a part.

1) Mirror your half chain ring to create a full one.   Select the

   Mirror icon. Select the **zx plane** as your Mirroring element:.   Read the *Status Bar* for help.

(**Problems?** If you get an error when trying to mirror the object, check to make sure that the bottom line of Sketch.2 (the tooth) goes completely below Pad.1.)

2) Enter the **Sketcher** on the **zx plane**.

3) Draw and **Constrain** the following **Rectangle**.

4) **Exit** the *Sketcher* and create a **Groove** using the sketch that travels *360 deg* using the **HDirection** as the Axis.

5) Enter the **Sketcher** on the front face of the part. Draw and constrain the following sketch. The length of the lines have to be long enough to go past the two circles, but the length beyond that doesn't matter.

6) Use the **Quick Trim** command to create a slot from the lines and circles previously draw.

7) Apply **0.09 in** radii **Corners** to the four sharp corners of the slot.

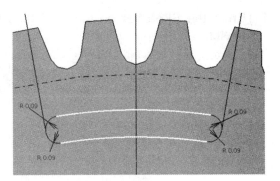

8) **Exit** the Sketcher and **Pocket** 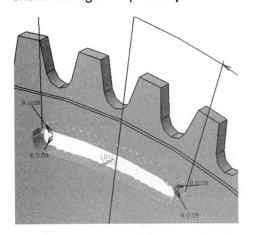 the sketch using the option **Up to last**.

9) **Propagate**.

10) Create a **Circular Pattern** of the slot creating **12** instances spaced **30 deg** apart. Use the top of the tooth (as before) as the reference element.

11) Enter the **Sketcher** on the front face of the part. Draw and constrain the following sketch.

12) Use the **Quick Trim** command to create the two shapes shown from the lines and circles previously draw.

13) **Exit** the Sketcher and

Pocket ⬜ the sketch using the option **Up to last**.

14) Mirror Pocket.2. Select the **Mirror** icon and then select **Pocket.2** in the specification tree. Select the **zx plane** as your Mirroring element:. Read the *Status Bar* for help.

15) **Propagate**.

16) Enter the **Sketcher** on the front face of the part. Draw and constrain the following sketch.

17) **Exit** the Sketcher and **Pocket** the sketch using the option **Up to last**.

0.25

0.125

R0.625

0.75

Section 3: Creating rectangular patterns.

1) **Propagate**.

2) Enter the **Sketcher** on the front face of the part. Draw and constrain the following sketch.

3) **Exit** the Sketcher and **Pocket** the sketch using the option **Up to last**.

4) Create a rectangular pattern of the rectangular slot that produces 2 rows 5 slots along the arm.

Select the **Rectangular Pattern** ▦ icon. In the *Rectangular Pattern Definition* window select the **First Direction** tab and fill in the following fields;
- Parameters: **Instance(s) & Spacing**
- Instance(s): **5**
- Spacing: **0.5 in**
- Reference element: select the front face of the part
- Object: **Pocket.4** (The pocket associated with the rectangular pocket).

Select the **Second Direction** tab and fill in the following fields;
- Parameters: **Instance(s) & Spacing**
- Instance(s): **2**
- Spacing: **0.125 in**
- Reference element: select the front face of the part
- Object: **Pocket.4**

5) Edit *Sketch.7* (the sketch associated with the rectangular slot) and change the height of the rectangle from 0.063 in to **0.094 in**.

6) **Exit** the Sketcher. Notice that all the rectangular slots in the array update based on the original.

7) Right click on RectPattern.1 in the specification tree and select **RectPattern.1 object – E̲xplode...** We have just broken the connection between the array elements. Notice that the RectPattern.1 feature is now broken up in to 10 individual pocket features.

8) Edit *Sketch.7* and change the height of the rectangle back to **0.063 in**.

9) **Exit** the Sketcher. Notice that only the Sketch.7 updates. The other slots are unaffected.

Section 4: Transformations.

When performing the transformations in this section, click on *Yes* in the *Question* window when prompted to (If one appears).

1) **Propagate**.

2) Scale the thickness of the Sprocket by a factor of 2.

Select the **Scale** icon and set the reference to be the **yz plane** and the ratio to be **2**.

3) Scale the part by *0.5* using the **xy plane** as a reference.

4) **Rotate** the part by *45 deg* using the **X Axis** as the rotation axis.

5) Select the **Undo/Redo Overview** icon. Undo all the transformations performed in this section.

Chapter 3:
PART DESIGN

Tutorial 3.8: Boolean Operations

FEATURED TOPICS & COMMANDS

THE BOOLEAN OPERATIONS TOOLBAR..2

BODIES TOOLBAR...2

LOCAL AXIS 3

TUTORIAL 3.8 START 3

    Section 1: Inserting a new part body. 3

    Section 2: Boolean operations..4

    Section 3: Local axes. 9

PREREQUISITE KNOWLEDGE & COMMANDS

- The *Sketcher* workbench and associated commands
- Editing a preexisting sketch
- Pads and Shafts
- Creating reference planes
- The *Transformation* toolbar
- Rotating the part using the mouse or compass

THE BOOLEAN OPERATIONS TOOLBAR

Boolean operations allow you to create parts from individual solids. The *Boolean Operations* toolbar is not, by default, active. To activate this toolbar click on **View - Toolbars** and then click on **Boolean Operations**. The commands located in the *Boolean Operations* toolbar, reading from left to right are

- Assemble: Assembling is a Boolean operation integrating 3D shape specifications. It allows you to create complex geometry. You can assemble the bodies and the resulting shapes look different depending on your specifications.
- Boolean Operations sub-toolbar
  - Add: Adding a body to another one means uniting them and creating a single body.
  - Remove: This command removes the intersecting volume of one body from another. The first body is then deleted.
  - Intersect: This command removes everything except the volume that is created when two bodies intersect.

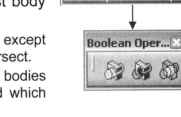

- Union Trim: This command allows you to add to bodies together while specifying which parts to keep and which parts will be trimmed.
- Remove Lump: This command allows you to reshape a body by removing material.

BODIES TOOLBAR

The *Bodies* toolbar is located in the Insert toolbar. The *Insert* toolbar is not, by default, active. To activate this toolbar click on **View - Toolbars** and then click on **Insert**.

When you create a solid distant from your original pad, it is still considered to be the same part. If you move one, the other moves. In the specification tree, these two pads are under the same PartBody. In some instances, it is desirable to create a solid that can be moved and transformed independently of the other solids that already exist. In order to accomplish this, a new

body has to be inserted. The *Body* command, which inserts a new body, is located in the *Bodies* toolbar.

When your part drawing includes several bodies, you can then associate these bodies in different ways (see the Assemble, Add, Union Trim, Intersect, Remove and Remove Lump commands) to obtain the final shape of the part.

LOCAL AXIS

The *Axis System* command is used to create a coordinate system away from the three original coordinate planes. The origin and axis directions may be defined. This new coordinate system may also be rotated.

TUTORIAL 3.8 START

The part modeled in this tutorial is shown below. It is created using the three main Boolean Operations (Add, Intersect, and Remove). New part bodies are inserted frequently to allow independent transformations.

Section 1: Inserting a new part body.

1) Start a **New 3D Part** name it *T38Handle* and, make your **PartBody** the **In Work Object**, change your **units** to **Millimeters**, and enter the **Sketcher** 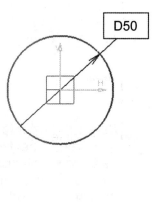 on the **zx plane**.

2) Draw and **Constrain** the **Circle** shown. The center of the circle is located at the origin.

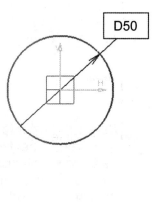

3) **Exit** the *Sketcher* and **Pad** the sketch **30 mm** in <u>both directions</u>.

4) Activate the *Insert* toolbar (**View - Toolbars - Insert**) .

5) Make your **PartBody** the **In Work Object**.

6) Insert a new body using the **Body** command. *Body.2* will automatically become the *In Work Object*.

7) Enter the **Sketcher** on the **yz plane**. Draw and **Constrain** the **Circle** shown. The center of the circle is located at the origin.

8) **Exit** the *Sketcher* and **Pad** the sketch **30 mm** in both directions. Your specification tree should look like the one shown.

D50

Section 2: Boolean operations.

1) Activate your Boolean operations toolbar if not already active. At the top pull down menu, select **View – Toolbars – Boolean Operations**.

2) Deselect all.

3) Select the **Intersect** icon and select the two cylindrical part bodies either in the tree or by selecting the bodies themselves. Select **OK** in the Intersect window. (Note: You need to select *Body.2* first.)

4) Make your **PartBody** the **In Work Object**.

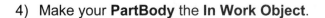

5) Insert a new body using the **Body** command.

6) Enter the **Sketcher** on the **zx plane**. Draw and **Constrain** the **Circle** shown. The center of the circle is located at the origin.

7) **Exit** the *Sketcher* and **Pad** the sketch **70 mm** in both directions. Your specification tree should look like the one shown.

8) Select the **Translate** icon. Select **Yes** in the *Question* window. Translate Body.3 **10 mm** in the **Z Axis** direction.

9) Deselect all.

10) Select the **Add** icon and add **Body.3** to the original **PartBody**.

11) **Propagate**.

12) Make your **PartBody** the **In Work Object** and insert a new **Body** .

13) Enter the **Sketcher** on the **xy plane**. Draw

   and **Constrain** the **Oriented Rectangle**
   as shown.

14) **Exit** the *Sketcher* and **Pad** the sketch *30 mm* in both directions.

15) **Remove** Body.4 from the original PartBody.

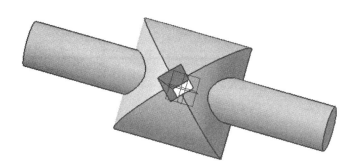

16) **Propagate**.

17) Make your **PartBody** the **In Work Object** and insert a new **Body** .

18) Enter the **Sketcher** on the end of the shaft.

Sketch face

Face/Translate.1/Body.3

19) **3D Project Elements** the end of the shaft as a **Construction Element**.

20) Draw and **Constrain** the **Axis** and **Arc** shown.

21) **Exit** the *Sketcher* and **Shaft** the sketch **360°**.

D30

22) **Translate** *Body.5* (the sphere) **10 mm** in the **Y Axis** direction.

23) Make **Body.5** the **In Work Object** and insert a new **Body**.

Translate Definition

Vector Definition: Direction, distance
Direction: Y Axis
Distance: 10mm

OK   Cancel

24) Enter the **Sketcher** on the **yz plane**. Draw and **Constrain** the **Axis** and **Profile** shown.

25) **Exit** the *Sketcher* and **Shaft** the sketch *360°*.

26) Make **Body.6** the **In Work Object** and then **Add** Body.5 to Body.6.

27) **Propagate**.

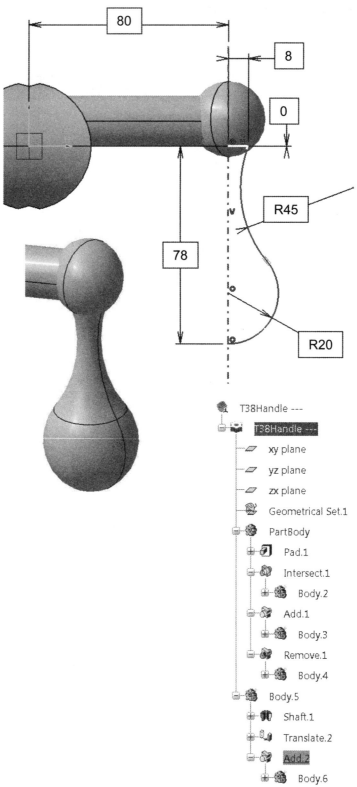

Section 3: Local axes.

1) Create a new **Plane** that is offset *80 mm* from the **zx plane**.

2) In the *Tools* toolbar, select the **Axis System**

   icon. In the *Axis System Definition* window, fill in the following fields;
   - Y axis: select the new plane (Plane.1)
   - Z axis: select the **xy plane**. (Note: The new axes will be perpendicular to the plane selected to define them.)

3) **Rotate** the handle grip (Body.5+Body.6) by *20°* using the newly created **X axis** as the rotation axis.

4) **Mirror** the handle using the **zx plane** as the mirroring element.

5) **Add** the handle (Body.5) to the main PartBody.

6) At completion, the specification tree should look similar to that shown on the right.

7) **Propagate**.

Chapter 3:
PART DESIGN

Tutorial 3.9: Material Properties

FEATURED TOPICS & COMMANDS

APPLYING AND MODIFYING MATERIAL PROPERTIES...2

TUTORIAL 3.9 START 2

    Section 1: Applying Material. 2

    Section 2: Part properties. 5

    Section 3: Add a new material 6

    Section 4: Text.. 8

PREREQUISITE KNOWLEDGE & COMMANDS

- The *Sketcher* workbench and associated commands
- Editing a preexisting sketch
- Pads
- Rotating the part using the mouse or compass

APPLYING AND MODIFYING MATERIAL PROPERTIES

A specific material may be assigned to your part by using the *Materials Palette* command. There are only a few predefined materials available to choose from, but CATIA allows you to create new materials. After a material has been assigned to the part, its properties may be modified to suit your particular needs. This is done by double clicking on

the various domains under the material in the specification tree. Once the correct material properties have been assigned to your part, the part properties may be obtained

by selecting the *Measure Inertia* command. This is located in the *Measure Tools* toolbar. This command gives you information on the part's volume, area, mass, and moments of inertia.

TUTORIAL 3.9 START

The part modeled in this tutorial is simple. It is only used as a base for learning about applying and modifying materials and analyzing part properties.

Section 1: Applying Material.

1) Start a **New 3D Part** name it *T39Block* and, make your **PartBody** the **In Work Object**, change your **units** to **Millimeters**, and enter the **Sketcher** on the **yz plane**.

2) Draw and **Constrain** the **Rectangle** shown.

3) **Exit** the *Sketcher* and **Pad** the sketch to a length of *50 mm*.

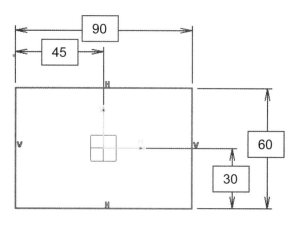

4) At the top pull down menu, select **<u>V</u>iew – Render St<u>y</u>le – <u>C</u>ustomize View**. In the *Custom View Modes* window, activate the **Materials** toggle.

5) To activate the *Materials Palette* enter the *Customize* window (**<u>T</u>ools - <u>C</u>ustomize...**), click on the **Commands** tab, select **All Commands** in the Categories field and the **Materials Palette** in the Commands field. Locate the *Measure Tools* toolbar . Click and drag the *Materials Palette* command into this toolbar.

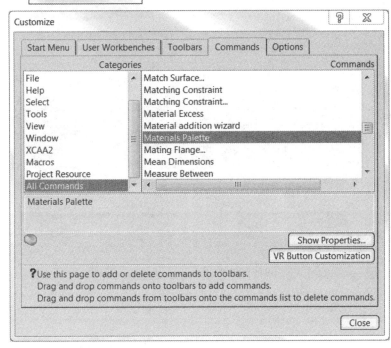

6) Click the **Materials Palette** command. If a *Did You Know* window appears, select **OK**. In the upper right corner a blue toolbar will appear. Select the **Thumbnail View** . Select the material **Aluminum** and then click on the *Block*. Notice that the material has been applied to your part. Try applying a few different materials and then close the *Materials Palette*.

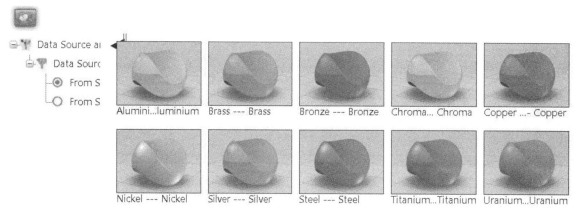

Alumini...luminium   Brass --- Brass   Bronze --- Bronze   Chroma... Chroma   Copper ...- Copper

Nickel --- Nickel   Silver --- Silver   Steel --- Steel   Titanium...Titanium   Uranium...Uranium

Section 2: Part properties.

1) Select the **Measure Inertia** 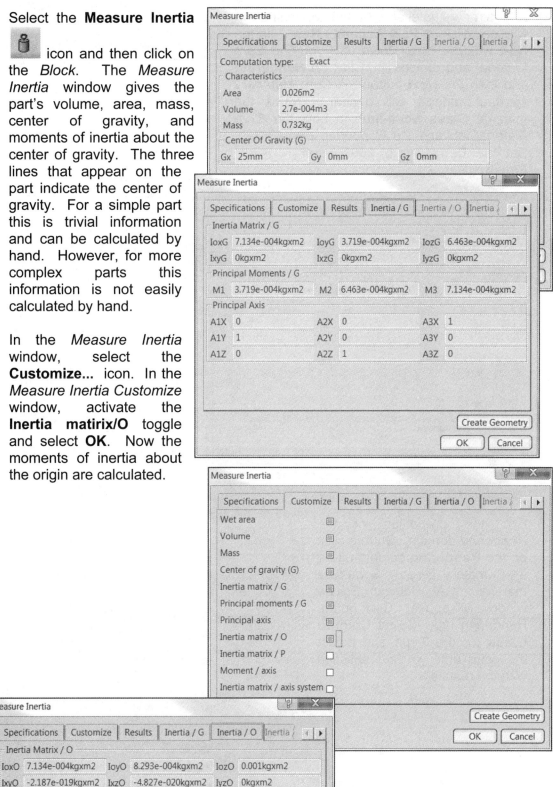 icon and then click on the *Block*. The *Measure Inertia* window gives the part's volume, area, mass, center of gravity, and moments of inertia about the center of gravity. The three lines that appear on the part indicate the center of gravity. For a simple part this is trivial information and can be calculated by hand. However, for more complex parts this information is not easily calculated by hand.

2) In the *Measure Inertia* window, select the **Customize...** icon. In the *Measure Inertia Customize* window, activate the **Inertia matirix/O** toggle and select **OK**. Now the moments of inertia about the origin are calculated.

Section 3: Add a new material

1) Add a new material. At the top pull-down window, click on **PLM Access - New...** In the *New* window, scroll down until you find *Core Material* and expand it. Click on **Rendering** and then the **Next** button. A *Core Material / Material* window will appear. Name the material **Glass Soda-lime** in both the *Core Material* tab and the *Rendering Domain* tab. Set the Density to **2500** kg/m^3. Select **Finish**.

2) Edit the properties of the *Rendering* domain. Double click on the **Rendering** domain under the main *Glass Soda-lime* material. A *Domain Edition* window will appear. Click on the Rendering tab. Select **Colored Glass** for the Type and adjust the color until you are satisfied with the results.

3) Add another domain to your *Glass* material. Right click on *Glass Soda-lime* and select **Add Domain**. In the Add Domain window, click on **ELFINI Linear Elastic domain** and then **OK**. In the *ELFINI Linear Elastic / Material Behavior*, Name the domain **Glass Soda-lime_ELFINI**.

4) Edit the *ELFINI* domain. Double click on **Glass Soda-lime_ELFINI**. In the *ELFINI Linear Elastic Domain* window, fill in the property values shown.

5) Add a **Drafting domain**. This is where you would set how section lines will look in the orthographic projection. Since CATIA does not have a hatch pattern for *Glass*, we will stick with the default pattern.

6) Get back into the **T39Block** window.

7) Apply the new *Glass* material to your block. Select the **Materials Palette** command. Select the **From Session** Data Source. Select **Glass Sode-lime** and then click on the *Block*.

Glass Soda-lime   Alumini...luminium

8) Use the **Measure Inertia** command to determine the mass of the *Block*. Notice that the *Glass Block* has a mass of 0.675 kg, where the *Aluminum Block* had a mass of 0.732 kg.

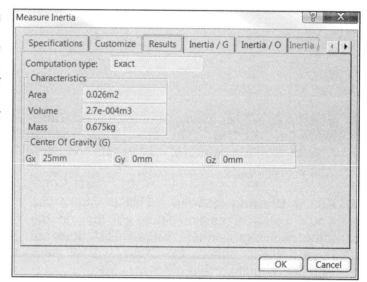

Section 4: Text

1) Make your block **Bronze**.

2) Enter **Sketcher** on the block's front face.

3) Pull out the *Predefined Profile* toolbar.

4) Select the **Text** command. In the *Text Creation* window, type the text you wish to place on the *Block*, select a Font and set the size.. If your text is long, you will need to create separate text entries. You can use the text paperclip to move your text into position. You can also apply dimensions. When your text is placed where you want it, **Exit** the *Sketcher*.

5) **Pocket** the text to a depth of **5** mm.

6) **Propagate**.

NOTES:

Chapter 3: Exercises

Exercise 3.1: This exercise can be performed after completing tutorial 3.1. Model the following parts.

a) Use at least one *Multiple Pad* when modeling this part.

b) Model this part using only one sketch and one *Multi-Pad* command.

Exercise 3.2: This exercise can be performed after completing tutorial 3.2. Model the following parts applying the appropriate constraints. Use the *Hole* command to create any holes, counterbores or threads.

a)

b)

Exercise 3.3: This exercise can be performed after completing tutorial 3.3. Model the following parts applying the appropriate constraints. Use the *Shaft* command to create the main solid.

a)

Ø100
⌴ Ø200
▽ 125

Ø400   Ø250   Ø250

100

225

250

NOTE: ALL FILLETS AND ROUND
R10 UNLESS OTHERWISE SPECIFIED

b)

2X Ø1.00
⌴ Ø1.75
▽ .38

Ø2.00   Ø3.50   Ø4.00

.12

.75

1.00

1.62

1.75

Exercise 3.4: This exercise can be performed after completing tutorial 3.4 and 3.5. Sketch the following parts applying the appropriate constraints. Apply *Edge Fillets* where necessary and at least on *Stiffener*. If you encounter problems applying an edge fillet, apply that one first before apply the others.

a)

NOTE: ALL FILLETS AND ROUNDS
R0.125 UNLESS OTHERWISE SPECIFIED

b)

NOTE: ALL FILLETS AND ROUNDS R3
UNLESS OTHERWISE SPECIFIED

Exercise 3.5: This exercise can be performed after completing tutorial 3.7. Model the following parts applying the appropriate constraints. Use the appropriate transformations in the *Part Design* workbench.

a)

R 5

4

(5)

1

22x9.5 ELLIPSE
(AT RIM)

Detail D
2XScale

24x11 ELLIPSE
(AT HUB)

64

32

D

6X3 KEYWAY

Ø 25

84

Ø 178 Ø 50

2X 2 × 45°

NOTE: ALL FILLET AND ROUNDS R3
UNLESS OTHERWISE SPECIFIED

b)

NOTES:

Chapter 4: ASSEMBLY DESIGN FUNDAMENTALS

INTRODUCTION

Chapter 4 focuses on CATIA's *Assembly Design* workbench. The reader will learn how to create and manage an assembly or product, and apply assembly constraints.

TUTORIALS CONTAINED IN CHAPTER 4

- Tutorial 4.1: Assembly Constraints and Advanced Commands
- Tutorial 4.2: Advanced Assembly

NOTES:

Chapter 4: ASSEMBLY DESIGN FUNDAMENTALS

Tutorial 4.1: Assembly Constraints and Advanced Commands

FEATURED TOPICS & COMMANDS

ASSEMBLY DESIGN WORKBENCH 2
PRODUCT STRUCTURE 2
INSERT MENU 3
THE ENGINEERING CONNECTION TOOLBAR 4
THE MEASURE AND 3D SECTION TOOLBAR 4
THE INTERFERENCE TOOLBAR 4
TUTORIAL 4.1 START 5
    Section 1: Creating the assembly 5
    Section 2: Wheel Sub-Assembly 9
    Section 3: Applying Engineering Connections 13
    Section 4: Measuring 17
    Section 5: Space Analysis 18
    Section 6: Rendering & Images 20

PREREQUISITE KNOWLEDGE & COMMANDS

- Entering workbenches
- The *Sketcher* workbench and associated commands
- The *Part Design* workbench and associated commands
- Moving and rotating parts with the compass

ASSEMBLY DESIGN WORKBENCH

The *Assembly Design* workbench allows you to design in the context of an assembly. You can add new or existing parts, or sub-assemblies to the root assembly. Parts can be positioned and constrained within the assembly. You can also analyze interferences between parts.

PRODUCT STRUCTURE

The product structure is best visualized by looking at the specification tree. Let's take, for example, the assembly of a machine vise. At the root is the product or assembly (Machine Vise). Under the assembly are parts (Base, Sliding Jaw, Jaw Plate, etc...), a subassembly (Handle Assembly), and constraints that are used to place parts in their functional positions. Notice that there are multiple copies of a single part. For example, there are 4 instances of Part11. Part11 was not drawn four different times; it was merely copied and pasted using the familiar CTRL+C and CTRL+V shortcuts. The root assembly and parts can be named by right clicking on the name and accessing the *Properties* window.

INSERT MENU

The Insert pull-down menu allows you to insert both new and existing *Parts* and *Products* and apply *Engineering Connections* between them. When you are inserting an existing part or subassembly, their corresponding files are not copied into the assembly. They are just referenced by the assembly. Some of these commands have corresponding toolbars. The commands located in the Insert pull-down menu are

Insert - New

- Product: This command allows you to insert a new product or subassembly into the root assembly.
- Product with: This command allows you to insert a new product or subassembly (CATProduct) into the root assembly with their associated *Drawing*, *Finite element* or *Mechanism* representations.
- 3D Part: This command allows you to insert a new part that will be designed on the fly while you are designing the assembly.
- 3D Shape: This command allows you to insert a new shape that will be designed from scratch while you are designing the assembly.
- 3D Drawing: This command allows you to insert a new *Drawing*.

Insert - Existing

- Product: This command is used when you want to add an existing assembly.
- 3D Part: This command is used when you want to add an existing part.
- 3D Shape: This command is used when you want to add an existing shape.
- 3D Drawing: This command is used when you want to add an existing drawing.

- Multi Instantiation toolbar: This toolbar contains commands that allow you to create instances or duplicates of a component.

THE ENGINEERING CONNECTION TOOLBAR

Engineering Connections are the constraints used to place each part into the assembly in its functional position. The general process for constraining the parts in an assembly is; fix one component in space, use the compass to move the other parts into their approximate position, position the parts precisely using the correct constraint(s), and then

update the assembly to move the parts into position. If a part(s) has been moved out of position, the update command may be used to move the part(s) back into position. The available *Engineering Connections* are shown in the figure. You will need to experiment with these connections to fully realize what they do.

THE MEASURE AND 3D SECTION TOOLBAR

The *Measure* toolbar contains commands that measure distances, angles, mass, volume, inertia, etc... of your assembly or individual geometric element. You can keep the result of your measurement as an element in your specification tree. The commands located in the *Measure* toolbar, reading left to right, are

- <u>Create a measure Item:</u> This command measures several physical parameters of an element such as area and perimeter.
- <u>Create a measure Between:</u> This command measures between two geometric elements.

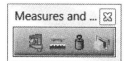

- <u>Create a measure Inertia:</u> This command measures physical parameters of a part or assembly. It will calculate the mass, volume, moments of inertia, and center of gravity among other things.
- <u>Sectioning:</u> This command allows you to manage product sections and cuts.

THE INTERFERENCE TOOLBAR

In the Interference toolbar, the "Clash" command allows you to analyzes any part interference. If there is an actual material interference between two parts, you will be warned.

TUTORIAL 4.1 START

The assembly modeled in this tutorial is used to cover assembly constraints and more advanced commands located in the *Assembly Design* workbench. Among other things we will apply material, calculate physical properties, analyze interferences, and create a section view.

Section 1: Creating the assembly

1) Enter the *Assembly Design* workbench (**PLM Access - Product...**). Name your product **T41ToyCar**. Remember, if necessary, add your name to the product name. Set your units to **Millimeters**.

2) Add a part to your assembly/product. At the top pull-down menu, select **Insert - New - 3DPart...** Name it **T41ToyCarBody** (both the part name and the physical representation.) (Note: If a *3DPart / Physical Product* window does not appear, click on *T41ToyCar*.)

3) **Propagate**

4) Expand your product in the specification tree until you can see the *T41ToyCarBody* *PartBody*. Double click on **PartBody**. This will automatically enter you into the *Part Design* workbench. You are now ready to draw. Make your **PartBody** the **In Work Object**.

5) Draw the following **Profile** on the **yz plane** and **Pad** it to a length of **98 mm**.

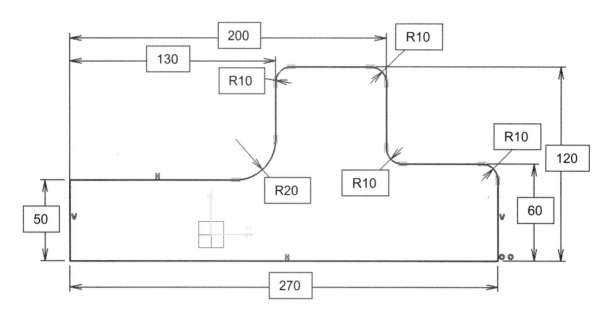

6) **Edge Fillet** the two side faces of the truck with a radius of **10 mm**.

7) Draw and **Pocket** the following sketches.

8) At the top pull-down menu, select **PLM Access - Propagate All...** This will bring up a *Propagate* window. This window gives you an overview of what is saved and what needs to be saved. Select **OK**. This will save all documents.

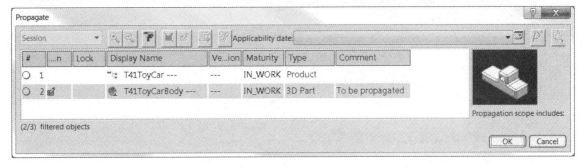

9) Enter the Sketcher on the top of the trucks bed. **Project** the face of the bed as a **construction element** and **Offset** it to the inside by *10 mm*. Turn the offset into a standard element. **Pocket** the offset to a depth of *30 mm*.

10) Make the *Body* PVC using the **Materials Palette** . If the *Materials Palette* is not active, you can activate it in the *Customize* window (**Tools - Customize...**). In the *Toolbars* tab, you can select the toolbar in which you want the command to go, select **Add commands...** and then select the command.

Section 2: Wheel Sub-Assembly

1) Double click on **T41ToyCar** in your specification tree to get back into the *Assembly Design* workbench.

2) **Propagate**

11) Add a sub-assembly/product to your assembly/product. At the top pull-down menu, select **Insert - New - Product...** Name it **T41ToyCarWheelAssembly** (Note: If a *Product / Physical Product* window does not appear, click on *T41ToyCar*.)

12) Make your **T41ToyCarWheelAssembly** active by double clicking on it.

13) Add a part to your sub-assembly/product. At the top pull-down menu, select **Insert - New - 3DPart...** Name it **T41ToyCarAxle** (both the part name and the physical representation.) (Note: If a *3DPart / Physical Product* window does not appear, click on *T41ToyCarWheelAssembly*.)

3) Double click on **T41ToyCarAxle** to enter the *Part Design* workbench. Make your **PartBody** the **In Work Object**.

4) Hide the car body. Right click on **T41ToyCarBody** and select **Hide/Show**.

5) Enter the **Sketcher** on the **zx plane** and sketch the axle. We will be creating a shaft that has symmetrical ends and is 150 mm long. Shown in the figure is one end.

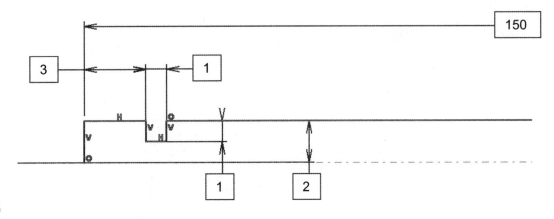

6)

7) **Shaft** the *Axle* and make it **Steel**.

8) Double click on **T41ToyCarWheelAssembly** and add. new **3DPart** to the Wheel Assembly and name it **T41ToyCarWheel**. Enter the Wheel's *Part Design* workbench and make its **PartBody** the **In Work Object**.

9) **Hide** the Axle.

10) Sketch the following profile on the **zx plane**. **Shaft** the sketch, and make the *Wheel* **Aluminum**.

R10

20

2.05

11) **Propagate All**

12) Use the same procedure as stated above to add a **New 3DPart** to the *Wheel Assembly* called **T41ToyCarSnapRing**. Enter the *Snap Ring's Part Design* workbench and draw the follow sketch on the **yz plane**. **Pad** the sketch to a length *0.8 mm*, and make the *Snap Ring* **Steel.**

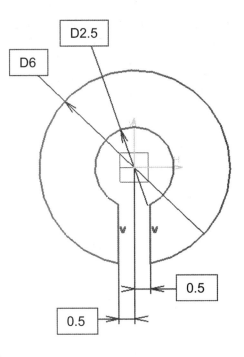

13) **Show** all the parts under the *Wheel Assembly*.

14) Double click on **T41ToyCarWheelAssembly** and move the parts, using the robot, to approximately the positions shown. To move a part using the robot, grab the robot at the origin and drag it onto the part you wish to move. Then use the axes to move it in the various directions.

15) Make a copy of the *Wheel* and *Snap Ring* (right click on the part and select **Copy** and then right click on the assembly and select **Paste**) and move them to the positions shown.

16) **Propagate All**.

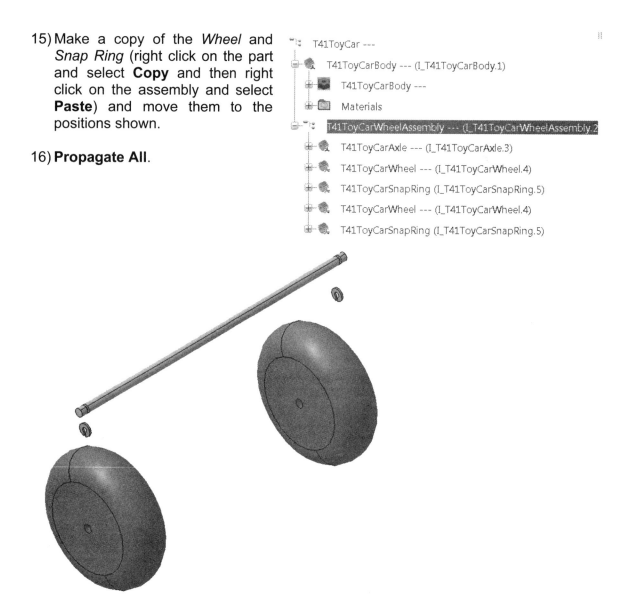

Section 3: Applying Engineering Connections

1) Apply an engineering connection between the wheels, snap rings and the axle that make them have a common axis. Select the **Engineering Connection**

icon. In the *Engineering Connection Definition* window, select the **Cylindrical** connection

Cylindrical . Select the axis of the *Axle* (you may have to move the mouse around a bit or even zoom in before it shows up) and then the axis the *Wheel*. Activate the Interference tab and select the **Check** radio button and select **No Clash**. Apply the Cylindrical connection between the other parts. (Note: If you get an interference warning when applying the connection to the Snap Ring, don't worry. We will be moving it later.)

the connection to the Snap Ring, don't worry. We will be moving it later.)

2) Locate the *Update* toolbar. It may be buried in the upper right corner. Select the **Update** icon to move the part into position. If an error window appears, take the robot and move one of the parts and then update again.

3) Move the parts using the robot so that each is visible. Notice that you can only move them axially because of the applied connections.

4) Apply a **Planar Connection** between the surface of the *Snap Rings* and the surface of the *Axle* groove as shown in the figure. When applying the connection, CATIA will ask you if this is a New connection or should it enrich an existing connection. Make it a **New connection**. Also, set the *Interference* to detect **Clashes**. Do this for both *Snap Rings*.

5) **Update** to move the part into position. If an error window appears, take the robot and move one of the parts and then update again.

6) We want to apply an Offset connection (a space) between the *Wheel* and *Snap Ring* as shown in the figure. This is done by applying a *Planar* connection and then modifying that connection. Apply a **Planar** connection between the outside *Wheel* surface and the inside *Snap Ring* surface. In the *Engineering Connection Definition* window, right click on the *Planar* icon under the Type field, select **Replace** and then select **Offset**. Right click on the number under the Value field and enter **1 mm**. Set the *Interferences* to **Check Clearance** at a minimum of **1 mm**. Repeat for the other *Wheel* and *Snap Ring*.

7) **Update** to move the part into position. If an error window appears, take the robot and move one of the parts and then update again.

8) Make a copy of the *Wheel Sub-Assembly*. Right click on *T41ToyCarWheelAssembly* and select **Copy**. Then, right click on *T41ToyCar* and select **Paste**. Move the sub-assembly with the robot as shown. To move the *Wheel Sub-Assembly Copy* you need to be in the *Toy Car* product.

9) **Show** the *ToyCarBody*.

10) Apply the following connections between the *Wheel Sub-Assemblies* and the *Body*

- **Fix** ⚓ Fix the *Body*. This part will be our anchor.

- Apply a **Cylindrical** connect 🌀 Cylindrical between the *Axles* and the holes in the *Body*.

- Apply an **Offset** connection 🔍 Offset between the inside surfaces of the *Wheel* and the side of the *Body* that is **1 mm**. If a warning window appear, click OK.

11) **Propagate All.**

Section 4: Measuring

1) Double click on **T41ToyCar** to make it the active item.

2) Locate the Measures and 3D Sections toolbar.

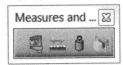

3) Select the **Create a measure Between** icon. In the *Measure Between* window, select *Axle's* axis as the `Selections`. A minimum distance of 210 mm will be calculated.

4) View the front of the car (use the *right side view* icon) and then select the **Create a measure Between** icon. Measure the distance between the outside surfaces of the *Wheels*. A minimum distance of 140 mm will be calculated.

5) Select the **Create a measure Item** icon. Select the **T41ToyCar** produce in the *Specification Tree*. Notice that the volume, area, and center of gravity are calculated. (Note: The center of gravity may be different from what is shown. This is because we did not constrain the car body with respect to the global axis.)

6) Select the **Create a measure Inertia** 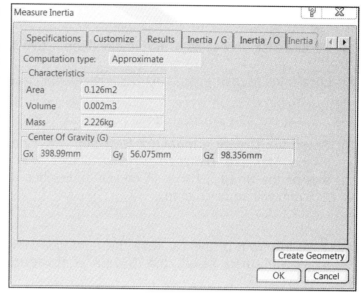 icon and then select the **T41CarBody** in the *Specification Tree.* Notice the physical parameters that are measured.

Section 5: Space Analysis

1) Make the root assembly active (*Toy Car*).

2) Select the **Create non persistent interference Simulation** icon located in the *Interference* toolbar. In Notice that the simulation detects only *Contact* and no *Clashes*.

#	Specification ▲	System status	Instance 1	Instance 2	Quantifier	Tolerance
1	Clash + Contact	Contact	T41ToyCarBody ---	T41ToyCarAxle ---	NA	0.2
2	Clash + Contact	Contact	T41ToyCarBody ---	T41ToyCarAxle ---	NA	0.2
3	Clash + Contact	Contact	T41ToyCarAxle ---	T41ToyCarWheel ---	NA	0.2
4	Clash + Contact	Contact	T41ToyCarAxle ---	T41ToyCar...apRing ---	NA	0.2
5	Clash + Contact	Contact	T41ToyCarAxle ---	T41ToyCarWheel ---	NA	0.2

3) Edit the car *Body* and change one of the axle holes to a diameter of **3 mm**. After you are done, re-enter the root assembly and re-apply the **Clash** command. Notice that now there is one clash. If you click on the **Clash** line it will show you where in the *Product* that the clash exists.

#	Speci...cation ▲	System status	Instance 1	Instance 2	Quantifier	Tolerance
1	Clash + Contact	Contact	T41ToyCarBody ---	T41ToyCarAxle ---	NA	0.2
2	Clash + Contact	Clash	T41ToyCarBody ---	T41ToyCarAxle ---	NA	0.2
3	Clash + Contact	Contact	T41ToyCarAxle ---	T41ToyCarWheel ---	NA	0.2
4	Clash + Contact	Contact	T41ToyCarAxle ---	T41ToyCarSnapRing ---	NA	0.2
5	Clash + Contact	Contact	T41ToyCarAxle ---	T41ToyCarWheel ---	NA	0.2

4) Change the axle hole diameter back to **4.1 mm**. After you are done, re-enter the root assembly.

5) Select the **Sectioning** icon located in the *Measures and 3D Section* toolbar. Play around with the options to obtain the following sections.

Section 6: Rendering & Images

1) Use the **Manipulation** 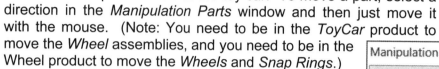 command, located in the *Move* toolbar, to create an exploded view of the toy car. To move a part, select a direction in the *Manipulation Parts* window and then just move it with the mouse. (Note: You need to be in the *ToyCar* product to move the *Wheel* assemblies, and you need to be in the Wheel product to move the *Wheels* and *Snap Rings*.)

2) At the top pull down menu, select **Tools – Image – Capture**. In the *Capture* window, select the **Capture Configuration** icon. Set the output parameters that you want. Choose a **Window area** by selecting the arrow to the right of the *Capture* icon. Select the **Capture** icon and draw a box around the exploded *ToyCar*. A *Capture Preview* window will appear showing your snap shot. If this is what you want, select the **OK**. In the *Save As* window, name your file and **Save**.

3) **Update** .

4) Click on the **Render** [icon] icon in the *Photo Studio* toolbar. In the *Render* window select the **Scene** [icon] icon. Choose a scene in which you want to place your car. The *Custom* tab allows you to set your lighting parameters. If you want to use one of your own pictures, select the *Background* checkbox and click the *Browse Image* icon. Once you have selected your scene, you can move, rotate and scale the *Toy Car* using the *Robot* and mouse buttons until you are happy with the results. Select **OK** to close the *Scene* window. Click on the **Rendering Options** [icon] icon and select the parameters that you want.

Then, select the **Define Render Area** [icon] icon to select the area you want to render. Finally **Render** [icon] and **Save** [icon] your rendering.

Render ? X
[icons]
Size: 6 x 4

Scene ? X
Predefined | Favorites | Custom
Default Lighting:

0.10
0.50
0.80
1.0

Background
Image: C:\Program Files\Dassault Syste
Stretch Image
Ground
Transparency: 0.00
Reflectivity: 0.00

OK | Cancel

Rendering Options ? X
Lens   Pinhole
Exposure   Sunny
Lighting   Realistic
Quality   High

OK | Ca

NOTES:

NOTES:

Chapter 4: ASSEMBLY DESIGN FUNDAMENTALS

Tutorial 4.2: Advanced Assembly

FEATURED TOPICS & COMMANDS

TUTORIAL 4.2 START 2

    Section 1: Setting up your product 3

    Section 2: Part 1 (Tool Post Body) 3

    Section 3: Part 2 (Wedge) 8

    Section 4: Part 3 (Bolt) 9

    Section 5: Part 4 through Part 9 10

    Section 6: Duplicating parts..19

    Section 7: Applying assembly constraints 20

PREREQUISITE KNOWLEDGE & COMMANDS

- Entering workbenches
- The *Sketcher* workbench and associated commands
- The *Part Design* workbench and associated commands
- Moving and rotating parts with the compass

TUTORIAL 4.2 START

The assembly and parts modeled in this tutorial are shown in the figures below. The main objective of this tutorial is to practice using the product structure and assembly constraints. However, assemblies are made up of parts that must fit together and fasten. Therefore, the parts modeled in this tutorial have toleranced dimensions and threads.

PART #	PART NAME	REQ'D	MAT
1	TOOL POST BODY	1	CI
2	WEDGE	1	SAE 1045
3	BOLT	1	SAE 1040
4	TOOL POST SCREW	2	SAE 1040
5	ADJUSTING SCREW	1	SAE 1040
6	HEX NUT	1	–
7	SET SCREW	2	SAE 1040
8	WASHER	1	SAE 1040
9	WASHER	1	SAE 1040
10	ADJUSTING NUT	1	SAE 1040

Section 1: Setting up your product

1) Start a **New Product** and name it **T42ToolPost** and set your units to **Inches** (**Tools – Options...**).

Section 2: Part 1 (Tool Post Body)

NOTE: ALL FILLETS AND ROUNDS R.06
UNLESS OTHERWISE SPECIFIED

1) Insert a New **3D Part** named **T42ToolPostBody**.

2) Expand the specification tree until you can see the *Bodies PartBody*. Double click on **PartBody**. This will automatically enter you into the *Part Design* workbench.

3) Make your **PartBody** the **In Work Object**.

4) Draw the right side profile of *Part1* on the **zx plane** as shown and **Pad** it to the appropriate length.

5) **Fillet** the appropriate edges.

6) Draw and **Pocket** the slot in the front of *Part1*. (Hint: Projecting the part edges will help.)

7) Create the **Hole** that travels from top to bottom. Notice that this hole is toleranced. Position the sketch before filling in the information. To access the *Limit of Size Definition* window click on the **Tolerance** icon. Note, the tolerance annotation shown on the CATIA part will be in metric ($\varnothing$12.7 +0.1 to +0.05). This can be changed by entering the dimension's **Properties** window and setting the Main Value to **NUM.DINC** and the Precision to **0.001**.

Limit of Size Definition

Tolerance
- ○ General Tolerance
  - Standard :
  - Tolerance :
- ● Numerical values
  - Upper Limit : 0.004in
  - ☐ Symmetric Lower Limit
  - Lower Limit : 0.002in
- ○ Tabulated values
  - H7
- ○ Single limit
  - ● MIN ○ MAX
  - Delta / nominal : 0in
- ○ Information

Options
- Envelop Condition : Ⓔ
- Statistical Tolerancing : ⓢⓣ

OK   Cancel

Hole Definition

Tolerance icon

Extension | Type | Thread Definition

Up To Last

Diameter : 0.5in

Depth : 4.5625in

Limit : No selection

Offset : 0in

Positionning Sketch

Direction
Reverse
☑ Normal to surface
No selection

Bottom
Flat
Angle : 120deg

OK

Properties

Current selection : Linear Size.1/Dimensions/Annotation Set.1

Graphic | 3D Annotation | Dimension Texts | Value | Tolerance | Di

Dimension Type
Projected dimension   ☐ Driving

Value Orientation
Reference: Dimension Line ▼ Position: Auto ▼
Orientation: Parallel ▼ Offset: 2.000 mm
Angle: 0.000 deg

Dual Value
☐ Show dual value   Below ▼

Format

	Main value	Dual value
Description: ❶	NUM.DINC ▼ ❸	NUM.DIMM ▼
Display:	1 factor ▼	1 factor ▼
Format:	Decimal ▼	Decimal ▼
Precision:	0.001 ▼	0.01 ▼

☐ Fake Dimension
○ Numerical   ● Alphanumerical
Main Value: 0.500 in   *Fake*

More...

OK   Apply   Close

8) Create the two threaded **Holes** on the top. The thread note is 7/16 – 14 UNC – 3B. The `Thread Diameter:` (major diameter) is **7/16**, the `Hole Diameter:` (tap drill) is **0.368** as obtained from a thread table, and the `Pitch:` is **1/14**.

9) Create the two threaded **Holes** in the front.

10) Create the Counter bored **Hole** in the side.

11) **Propagate All**.

Section 3: Part 2 (Wedge)

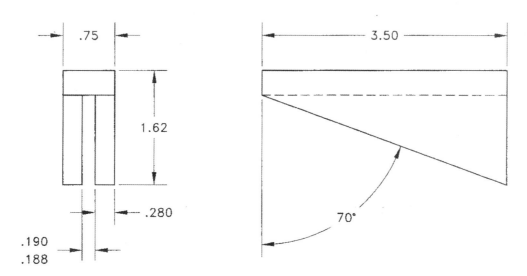

1) Double clicking on **T42ToolPost**, add a **New 3D Part** named **T42ToolPostWedge** and prepare to draw *Part2* the *Wedge*.

2) Notice that one of the *Wedge's* dimensions is toleranced. To create a toleranced dimension, right click on the `Value` field in the *Constraint Definition* window and select **Add tolerance ....** When the *Tolerance* window appears, enter the max. and min. tolerance values. Notice that after the tolerance is applied the dimension reads 0.19 - 0.002.

3) **Propagate All**.

Section 4: Part 3 (Bolt)

1) Double clicking on **T42ToolPost**, add a **New 3D Part** named **T42ToolPostBolt** and prepare to draw *Part3* the *Bolt*.

2) Notice that the bolt shaft is toleranced. Use a basic size of 0.500 and the same procedure as before to apply the tolerance. The shaft also has threads.   Use the

   Thread/Tap command to apply them.

3) **Propagate All**.

Section 5: Part 4 through Part 9

1) Model parts 4 through 9 and add them to the assembly as before. Note that parts 6, 7, and 8 are standard parts. Key steps for creating each part, the final specification tree, and final part are shown in the series of figures given below.

Part 4 (Tool Post Screw)

Part 5 (Adjusting Scew)

5/16 — 18 UNC — 3A

.03 X 45°

ø.38

.25

2.00

4.25

.186
.184

T42ToolPost ---
- T42ToolPostBody --- (I_T42ToolPostBody.1)
- T42ToolPostWedge --- (I_T42ToolPostWedge.1)
- T42ToolPostBolt --- (I_T42ToolPostBolt.2)
- T42ToolPostScrew --- (I_T42ToolPostScrew.3)
- T42ToolPostAdjustingScrew (I_T42ToolPostAdjustingScrew.4)
  - T42ToolPostAdjustingScrew
    - xy plane
    - yz plane
    - zx plane
    - Geometrical Set.1
    - PartBody
      - Pad.1
      - Pad.2
      - Thread.1
      - Pocket.1

Part 6 (Hex Nut)

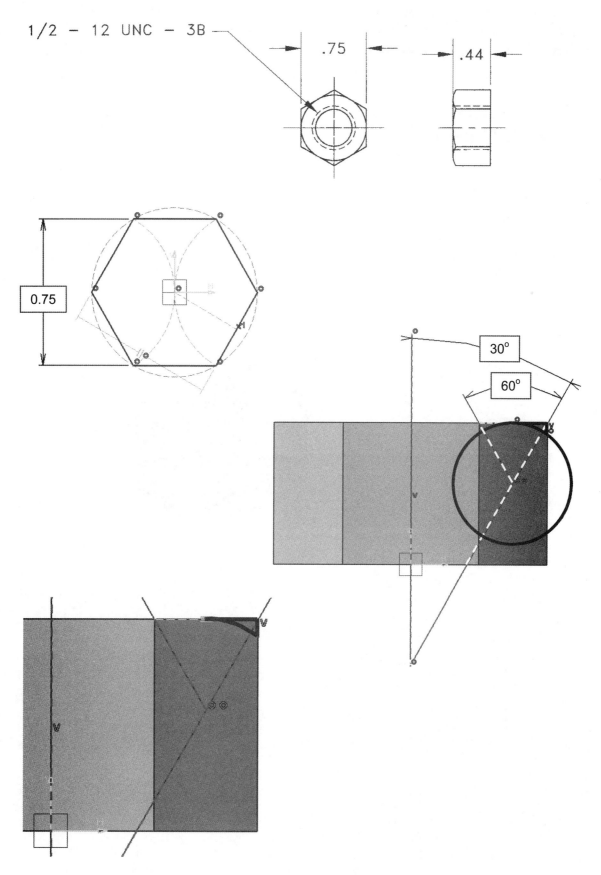

1/2 - 12 UNC - 3B

.75

.44

0.75

30°

60°

Part 7 (Set Screw)

.03 X 45°

1/4 — 20 UNC — 3A

.05 X ⌵.06

.05 SPHERICAL

1.53

1.53

0.125   0.03   45°   45°   R0.2

0.05

T42ToolPost ---

T42ToolPostBody --- (I_T42ToolPostBody.1)

T42ToolPostWedge --- (I_T42ToolPostWedge.1)

T42ToolPostBolt --- (I_T42ToolPostBolt.2)

T42ToolPostScrew --- (I_T42ToolPostScrew.3)

T42ToolPostAdjustingScrew --- (I_T42ToolPostAdjustingScrew.4)

T42ToolPostHexNut --- (I_T42ToolPostHexNut.5)

T42ToolPostSetScrew (I_T42ToolPostSetScrew.6)

T42ToolPostSetScrew

xy plane

yz plane

zx plane

Geometrical Set.1

PartBody

Shaft.1

Pocket.1

Thread.1

Part 8 (Washer)

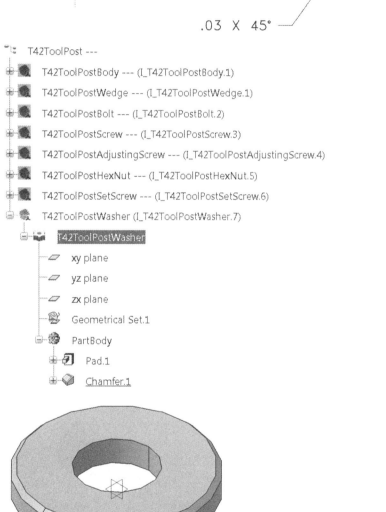

Part 9 (Slotted Washer)

Part 10 (Adjusting Nut)

5/16 — 18 UNC — 3B

R.06

MEDIUM KNURL

.03 X 45° BOTH SIDES

ø1.06 ø.62

.31

.62

Hole Definition

Extension | Type | **Thread Definition**

☐ Threaded

Bottom Type

Type: Dimension ▾

Bottom Limit: No selection

Thread Definition

Type: No Standard ▾

Thread Diameter: 0.313in

Hole Diameter: 0.257in

Thread Depth: 0.625in

Hole Depth: 0.62in

Pitch: 0.056in

◉ Right-Threaded ○ Left-Threaded

OK | Cancel | Preview

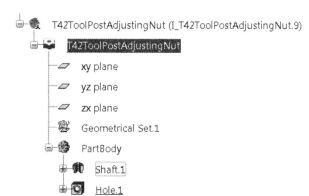

T42ToolPostAdjustingNut (I_T42ToolPostAdjustingNut.9)

T42ToolPostAdjustingNut

xy plane

yz plane

zx plane

Geometrical Set.1

PartBody

Shaft.1

Hole.1

Section 6: Duplicating parts

1) After inserting and drawing all the parts, **Show** all the parts. Using the *Robot*, move them so that you can see all the part. (Remember: You have to be in the root assembly to move the individual parts.)

2) Notice that we are missing one *Tool Post Screw* and one *Set Screw*. To make copies, right click on **T42ToolPostScrew** in the specification tree and select **Copy**. Then, right click on **T42ToolPost** and select **Paste**. Repeat for the *Set Screw*.

```
T42ToolPost ---

    T42ToolPostBody --- (I_T42ToolPostBody.1)

    T42ToolPostWedge --- (I_T42ToolPostWedge.1)

    T42ToolPostBolt --- (I_T42ToolPostBolt.2)

    T42ToolPostScrew --- (I_T42ToolPostScrew.3)

    T42ToolPostAdjustingScrew --- (I_T42ToolPostAdjustingScrew.4)

    T42ToolPostHexNut --- (I_T42ToolPostHexNut.5)

    T42ToolPostSetScrew --- (I_T42ToolPostSetScrew.6)

    T42ToolPostWasher (I_T42ToolPostWasher.7)

    T42ToolPostSlottedWasher (I_T42ToolPostSlottedWasher.8)

    T42ToolPostAdjustingNut (I_T42ToolPostAdjustingNut.9)

    T42ToolPostScrew --- (I_T42ToolPostScrew.3)

    T42ToolPostSetScrew --- (I_T42ToolPostSetScrew.6)
```

Section 7: Applying assembly constraints

1) **Fix** 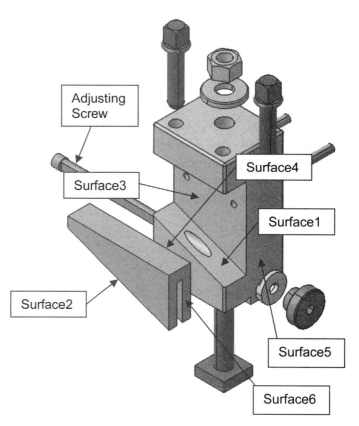 the *Tool Post Body* and then apply the appropriate **Engineering Connections** and **Interferences** to the rest of the parts.

2) Apply a **Planar** constraint between surface1 and surface2 as indicated in the figure.

3) Apply a **Planar** Constraint between surface3 and surface4 (the back side of the wedge) as indicated in the figure.

4) Apply an **0.5 Offset** constraint between surface5 and surface6.

5) **Update** though out the tutorial as necessary to check your connections.

6) Apply a **Cylindrical** constraint between the *Adjusting Screw* and the counterbored hole in the *Tool Post Body*.

7) Apply a **Planar** constraint between the bottom surface of the *Adjusting Screws* head (you will probably have to zoom in to be able to select it) and the bottom surface of the counterbored hole in the *Tool Post Body*.

8) Apply the appropriate **Cylindrical** constraints between the *Adjusting Screw*, and the *Slotted Washer* and *Adjusting Nut*. Remember to choose the axes and zoom in when necessary.

9) Apply the appropriate **Planar and** constraints between the *Wedge* and *Slotted Washer* and the *Slotted Washer* and the *Adjusting Nut*.

Adjusting Screw

Adjusting Nut

Slotted Washer

10) Use the appropriate constraints to place the two *Tool Post Screws*, the *Bolt*, the *Washer*, and the *Hex Nut* into their functional positions.

11) Apply **Cylindrical** constraints to the *Set Screws* and the holes in the *Tool Post Body*.

12) Create a **-0.125 Offset** constraint between the end of the *Set Screws* and surface3.

13) **Propagate All**.

14) Do a **Clash** ![icon] simulation. You should find the following *Clashes*. This is because they are threaded features. Everything else should list *Contact*. If you have more *Clashes* than is listed, your connections need to be adjusted.
   - Tool Post Screw and Body (both screws)
   - Set Screw and Body (both screws)
   - Bolt and Body/Hex Nut
   - Adjusting Screw and Adjusting Nut

Chapter 4: Exercises

Exercise 4.1: This exercise can be performed after completing the tutorials presented in chapter 4. Model and constrain the following parts and assembly.

Exercise 4.2: This exercise can be performed after completing the tutorials presented in chapter 4. Model and constrain the following parts and assembly.

PART #	PART NAME	REQ'D	MAT
1	TROLLEY WHEEL	2	1020 STEEL
2	SIDE PLATE	2	HRS
3	CROSS HEAD	1	CRS
4	AXLE	2	CRS
5	ADJUSTING SHIM	2	HRS
6	KEEPER PLATE	2	CRS
7	BALL BEARING	2	–
8	AXLE SNAP RING	2	SPRING STEEL
9	WHEEL SNAP RING	4	SPRING STEEL
10	7/8 HEX HEAD BOLT	2	–
11	7/8 HEX HEAD NUT	2	–
12	7/8 PLAIN WASHER	8	–
13	ROUND HD MACH SCR	4	–

DRAWN BY: KIRSTIE PLANTENBERG	# OF SHEETS: 1	SHEET #: 8		SCALE: 1:2.5
PART NAME: TROLLEY	PART #: –	MAT: –		REQ'D: 1

AXLE SNAP RING
SPRING STEEL

8

TROLLEY WHEEL
1020 STEEL

1

WHEEL SNAP RING
SPRING STEEL

SPRING STEEL

9

DEPARTURE
BALL BEARING
#99504

7

AXLE
CRS

4

Part#1

Part#1, Part#8 and Part#9

Part#4 and Part#7

Part#2 and Part#6

Part#3 and Part#5

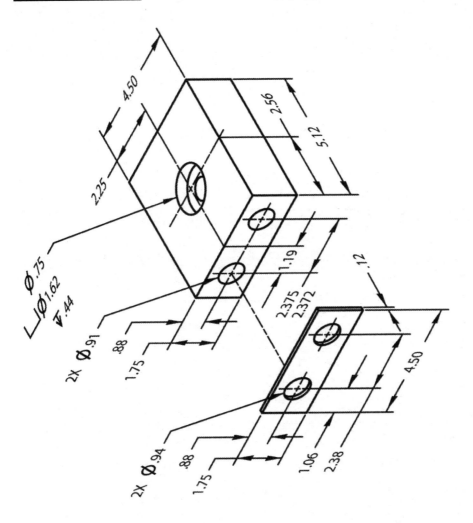

NOTES:

Chapter 5: DRAFTING FUNDAMENTALS

INTRODUCTION

Chapter 5 focuses on CATIA's *Drafting* workbench. The reader will learn how to create a simple orthographic projection and associated dimensions.

TUTORIALS CONTAINED IN CHAPTER 5

- Tutorial 5.1: Generative Drafting

NOTES:

NOTES:

Chapter 5:
DRAFTING FUNDAMENTALS

Tutorial 5.1: Generative Drafting

FEATURED TOPICS & COMMANDS

THE DRAFTING WORKBENCH 2

THE VIEWS TOOLBAR..2

THE ANNOTATIONS TOOLBAR 3

TUTORIAL 5.1 START 4

    Section 1: Modeling the part...5

    Section 2: Creating standard views 5

    Section 3: Creating section views..10

    Section 4: Cleaning up the views 11

    Section 5: Dimensioning...14

PREREQUISITE KNOWLEDGE & COMMANDS

- Entering workbenches
- The *Sketcher* workbench and associated commands
- The *Part Design* workbench and associated commands

THE DRAFTING WORKBENCH

The *Drafting Workbench* allows you to create an orthographic projection or drawing directly from a *3D Part* or *Assembly*. A *Drawing* contains a structure listing similar to a specification tree. The structure listing shows all the sheets and views contained in the document. CATIA enables you to create *generative views* that are associative with the *3D Part*, and to create *drawn views* which are not associative.

THE VIEWS TOOLBAR

The commands located in the *Views* toolbar enable you to create a variety of views and view configurations. The sub-toolbars located within the *Views* toolbar, reading left to right, are

- Projections toolbar: The *Projections* toolbar contains commands that allow you to create different types of views. The commands, reading from left to right, are; *Front View, Unfolded View, View from 3D, Projection View, Auxiliary View, Isometric View*.
- Sections toolbar: This toolbar contains commands that allow you to create a variety of section and cut views.
- Details toolbar: The *Details* toolbar contains commands that allow you to create views that are a small portion of an existing view. The detail view is usually drawn at an increased scale.
- Clippings toolbar: The command located in the *Clippings* toolbar allow you to create removed views or removed section views. This is a small area of the part that is shown apart from the original view and is usually shown at an increased scale.
- Break view toolbar: The commands located in the *Break view* toolbar allow you to break the part in a specified location. This is usually done to save drawing space. The missing section of the part is usually uninteresting and not worth showing. There is also a command that enables you to create a broken out section.
- Wizard toolbar: This toolbar contains commands that allow you to select from several predefined view configurations or to define your own custom configuration. Reading from left to right, the commands are; '*View Creation Wizard*', which allows you to create custom view configurations, '*Front, Top and Left*', '*Front, Bottom and Right*', and '*All Views*'.

THE ANNOTATIONS TOOLBAR

The commands located in the *Annotation* toolbar allow you to create drawing annotations including dimensions and tolerances. The sub-toolbars, reading from left to right, are

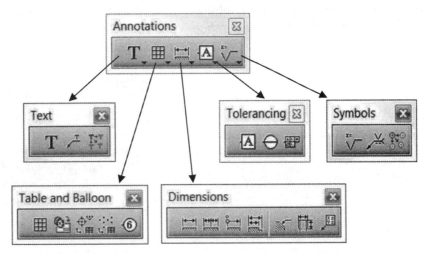

- Text toolbar: The *Text* toolbar contains commands that allow you to create text and leader dimensions.
- Table and Balloon: The Table and Balloon toolbar contains commands assotiated with assembly drawing. For example, you can create *Bill of Materials*, other tables and identification *Balloons*.
- Dimensions toolbar: The *Dimensions* toolbar contains commands that allow you to manually create dimensions. The commands, reading from left to right, are; *Dimensions, Chained Dimensions, Cumulated Dimensions, Stacked Dimensions, Chamfer Dimensions, Thread Dimensions, Coordinate Dimensions*.
- Tolerancing toolbar: The *Tolerancing* toolbar contains commands that allow you identify *Datum Features*, *Datum Target* and to apply feature control frames with associated *GD&T* symbols.
- Symbols toolbar: The *Symbols* toolbar contains commands that allow you to add *Welding* and *Rough Surface* symbols to the drawing.

TUTORIAL 5.1 START

The part modeled in this tutorial is used to illustrate the basic commands available in the *Drafting* workbench. You will learn how to create an orthographic projection that contains a section view, and how to create and place dimensions.

Section 1: Modeling the part

1) Open a **New 3D Part**, name it **T51Jig**, set your units to **Millimeters** and make your **PartBody** the **In Work Object**.

2) Model the part shown on the previous page in the *Part Design* workbench and **Propagate**.

Section 2: Creating standard views

1) Make sure your part is in a similar position as shown in the *Tutorial Start* section. Your isometric view is based on the orientation of you solid model.

2) Create a new *Drawing* (**PLM Access - Drawing...**) and name it **T51Jig**. In the *Drawing / Physical Representation* window, select the **Drawing Information** tab and set the Standard to **ANSI** and the Sheet Style to **A ANSI**.

3) When the blank sheet appears, right click on **Sheet.1** in your structure listing (on the left) and select **Properties**. In the Properties window make sure that the **third angle standard** is active.

(**NOTE:** If you are searching for a Drawing file, you need to type **Drawing: *** in the Search field.)

4) Select the **View Creation Wizard** icon. In the *View Wizard (Step 1/2) Predefined Configuration* window, select the **Front, Top and Right** configuration icon. Select the **Next >** button. In the *View Wizard (Step 2/2): Arranging the Configuration* window, select the **Isometric view** icon and place the view as shown. Select the **Finish** button.

5) The *Status Bar* will read, *Select a reference plane on a 3D geometry*. At the top pull down menu, select **Window** and then your part drawing. Move your mouse over the front face of the part. An *Oriented Preview* window will appear in the corner showing you what the front view will look like. If this is acceptable, click the mouse.

6) Your sheet should contain the front view and areas for the top, right and isometric views. These are not necessary in their final positions. The *Status Bar* will read, *Click on the sheet to generate the view or redefine the view orientation using the arrows*. Look at the front view. If the orientation is not correct, you can use the blue circle with four arrows to reorient the front view. If the orientation is correct, click on the sheet.

7) After you accept the front view orientation by clicking on the screen, the other views will appear. The front view should be the view that is active (in a red border). If it is not active, double click on it. Move the front view towards the bottom left corner, and then move the other views as shown in the figure. To move a view, click on the view border and move the mouse. Notice that when you try to move the isometric view it is constrained by the location of the front view. Right click on the isometric view's border and select **<u>V</u>iew Positioning – <u>P</u>osition Independently of Reference View**. Then, move the isometric view to the position shown.

(**Problem?** If you have no view borders, activate the *Display View Frame as Specified for Each View* icon.)

8) **Propagate**.

9) Notice that none of the views contain hidden or center lines. Right click on the **Right view** identifier in the structure listing and select **Properties**. In the *Generation* tab of the *Properties* window, activate the **Hidden Lines, Center Lines,** and **Axis** toggles in the *Dress-up* area. Repeat for the front and top views.

Top view
Scale: 1:1

Front view
Scale: 1:1

Right view
Scale: 1:1

5.1 - 9

Section 3: Creating section views

1) Create a full section right side view. Make your front view active. Select the **Offset**

   Section ▦ icon. Choose the location of your cutting plane in your front view by selecting point1 as indicated in the figure and then double clicking at point2. A shaded view will appear. Place it to the right of the right side view and click. (Note: You will have to deactivate the *Snap to Point* if it is active.)

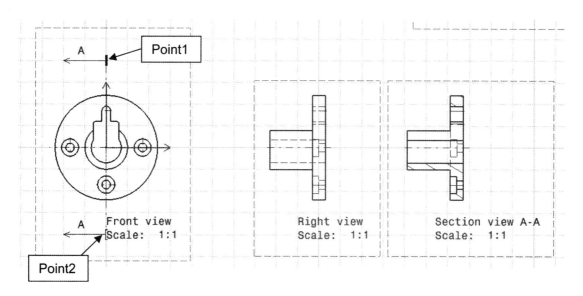

2) Change the look of the section lines. In the section view, double click on the section lines. In the *Properties* window click on the **Pattern** tab and change the angle to *45°* and the pitch to *1 mm*.

Section 4: Cleaning up the views

1) Delete the right side unsectioned view and the top view for these views are not needed. Right click on the border of the view and select **Delete**.

2) Notice that in the right side sectioned view there are two places where two lines (center and hidden) are coincident. According to drafting standards only one of those lines should be shown. Usually the center line would be deleted, but in this case the hidden lines have no reason for being there (they are used to show a fillet). Enter the *Properties* window for the right side view.   Deselect the **Fillet** toggle.

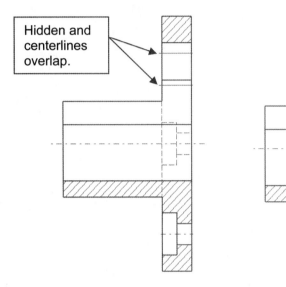

3) Section views usually do not contain hidden lines. Eliminate the hidden lines in the right side section view.

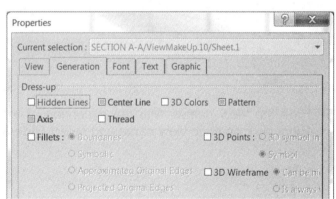

4) Change the properties of the cutting plane line. Right click on the cutting plane line and select **Properties**. In the *Properties* window, click on the **Call out** tab and set the line thickness to *3* and the line type to *5*. Set the length of the arrow line to *10 mm*. Set the arrow head type to solid, the length to *5 mm*, and the angle to *30°*.

5) Hide the view names with the exception of the *Section View* name **Section A-A**. Right click on each view name and select **Hide/Show**.

6) Change the scale of the views to 2:1. Right click on Sheet.1 and select **Properties**. In the *Properties* window set the scale to *2:1*.

7) Change the scale of the isometric view back to **1:1**.

8) **Propagate**.

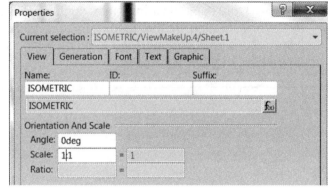

Section 5: Dimensioning

1) Make the right side view active by double clicking on its frame/border.

2) Draw a phantom line that indicates the full diameter of the hub. Draw two lines as indicated in the figure. Select both lines, right click, and select **Properties**. In the *Properties* window, set the line thickness to **1** and the line type to **5**.   Commands such as line, circle, etc… are located in the *Geometry Creation* toolbar. (Hint: Start with the short vertical line which is 2 mm long at an angle of 90 degrees.)

3) Place the linear dimensions in the right side view. Select the **Dimensions** icon, located in the *Annotations* toolbar / *Dimensions* sub-toolbar. Look up at the top and find the *Numerical Properties* toolbar. It should read **NUM.DIMM**. That means that your dimension values will be in millimeters. If it does not read *NUM.DIMM*, change it. Then, select *Line1* followed by *Line2*. Repeat, using a similar procedure, for the 26 mm dimension. Note: You can move the arrows in and outside of the extension lines by clicking on them. You can also drag the texts outside the extension lines. Move the *SECTION A-A* view name if it is in the way.

4) Follow the same procedure for the diameter dimensions (20, 48), however; after creating a dimension place a diameter symbol in front of the text.

5) Activate the front view by double clicking on it.

6) Draw a **Circle** that identifies the circle of centers of the counterbored holes. Right click on the circle and select **Properties**. Change the line type to **4** and the line thickness to **1**.

7) Use the **Dimensions** command to dimension the 3 diameter dimensions shown in the figure. Notice that the dimensions do not look like the dimensions shown in the figure. Select all 3 dimensions holding the Ctrl key and access the *Properties* window. In the **Dimension Line** tab change the following settings.

- `Representation:` **Two Parts**
- Deactivate the **Symbol 2** toggle.

Position the dimensions as shown. (Note: If the dimension landing disappears, you will need to activate the option in the *Text Properties* toolbar.

8) Notice that the dimension for the counterbored hole is not correctly stated. It shows only the diameter of the counterbore. Access the *Properties* window for that dimension. Select the **Value** tab and activate the **Fake Dimension** toggle. Enter a Main Value: of *4 mm*. This is the diameter of the hole. Select the **Dimension Text** tab. Enter *3X* in the top box of the Main Value field. This indicates that there are 3 counterbored holes.

9) We still need to add the counterbore diameter and depth. Select the **Text** T icon. Click your mouse under the ∅4 dimension. A *Text Editor* window will appear. At the top of the screen there should be a *Text Properties* toolbar. Click on the **Insert Symbol** icon and select the counterbore symbol, type a space, select the diameter symbol ∅ , and then type *8*. Hit **Shift-Enter** to start a new line. Select the deep symbol, and then type *3*.

10) Move the counterbore dimension and text into its proper position as shown in the figure. Hold the **Shift** key down while moving the counterbore text to avoid a jerky motion.

11) **Propagate**.

12) Dimension the rest of the linear **Dimensions** .

13) Add the radii dimensions using **Dimensions** . Click on the radius you wish to dimension and then before you place the dimension, right click and select **Radius Center**. Enter the dimension's *Properties* window to change the dimension appearance and add text. If you accidentally create a diameter dimension, right click on the dimension and *Swap to Radius*.

14) Locate the *Visualization* toolbar. Position your views and then deactivate the **Display View Frame as Specified for Each View** , **Sketcher Grid** and **Elements Analysis** icons. This should turn off all of the view frames.

15) **Propagate**.

NOTES:

Chapter 5: Exercises

Exercise 5.1: This exercise can be performed after completing the tutorials presented in chapter 5. Create a detailed drawing of the exercises presented in chapter 2 and 3. The detailed drawing should include the appropriate views as well as an isometric view. Include section views were necessary. Dimension the orthographic projection completely.

NOTES:

Chapter 6: GENERATIVE SURFACE DESIGN FUNDAMENTALS

INTRODUCTION

Chapter 6 focuses on CATIA's *Generative Surface Design* workbench. The reader will learn how to create basic wireframe surfaces and use them to create solids.

TUTORIALS CONTAINED IN CHAPTER 6

- Tutorial 6.1: Wireframe toolbar
- Tutorial 6.2: Surfaces toolbar
- Tutorial 6.3: Operations toolbar

NOTES:

NOTES:

Chapter 6: GENERATIVE SHAPE DESIGN FUNDAMENTALS

Tutorial 6.1: Wireframe toolbar

FEATURED TOPICS & COMMANDS

THE GENERATIVE SHAPE DESIGN WORKBENCH 2

THE WIREFRAME TOOLBAR 3

THE POINTS TOOLBAR 4

THE LINE-AXIS TOOLBAR 4

THE PLANES TOOLBAR.. 4

THE PROJECT-COMBINE TOOLBAR 5

THE CURVE OFFSET TOOLBAR... 5

THE CIRCLE-CONIC TOOLBAR 5

THE CURVES TOOLBAR 6

TUTORIAL 6.1 START 6

Section 1: Points and lines 7

Section 2: Splines... 9

Section 3: Surfaces 14

Section 4: Creating solids... 19

PREREQUISITE KNOWLEDGE & COMMANDS

- Entering workbenches
- The *Sketcher* workbench and associated commands
- The *Part Design* workbench and associated commands

THE GENERATIVE SHAPE DESIGN WORKBENCH

The *Generative Shape Design* workbench is very similar to the *Wireframe and Surface Design* workbench. You may do the tutorials within either workbench. The *Generative Shape Design* workbench is used to create complex wire frame profiles and surfaces. In the *Part Design* workbench we worked under a *PartBody* which contained features used to create a solid.

The general process for creating a wireframe object is as follows: enter the *Generative Shape Design* workbench, create wireframe geometry, create surfaces from existing geometry, modify and transform the surfaces (trim, join), enter the *Part Design* workbench, create a part body (solid), and modify the part using *Part Design* commands.

The *Generative Shape Design* workbench contains the following standard workbench specific toolbars.

- <u>Wireframe toolbar:</u> This toolbar contains commands used to create reference elements such as points, lines, and curves that will be used to create surfaces.

- <u>Surfaces toolbar:</u> Once the reference geometry is constructed, the commands located in the *Surfaces* toolbar are used to create the surfaces.

- <u>Operations toolbar:</u> The commands located in the *Operations* toolbar are used to modify and transform surfaces and reference elements.

- <u>Replications toolbar:</u> The commands located in the *Replication* toolbar are used to duplicate features such as points and planes.

- <u>Volumes toolbar:</u> The commands located in the *Volumes* toolbar are used to create and modify solids.

THE WIREFRAME TOOLBAR

The commands located in the *Wireframe* toolbar are used to create reference elements such as points, lines, and curves that will be used to build surfaces. The commands and sub-toolbars located in the *Wireframe* toolbar, reading left to right, are

- **The Points toolbar:** Contains command to create reference points relative to the origin, another point, a curve or a surface.
- **The Line-Axis toolbar:** Used to create lines, axes, and polylines.
- **Plane toolbar:** Allows you to create reference planes and points similar to that in the *Part Design* workbench. You can use planes as reference elements or cutting elements.
- **Project-Combine toolbar:** This command creates a projection of a point, curve, or surface onto a support element, usually a plane or surface.
- **Intersection:** This command creates a curve that follows the intersection of a surface with a specified element.
- **Curve Offset toolbar:** contains commands that allow you to create offset geometry based on a referenced curved.
- **The Circle-Conic toolbar:** Contains commands that will create circles, conics, corners (fillets), and connect curves.
- **The Curves toolbar:** Used to create splines, helixes, spirals, spines and isoparametric curves.

THE POINTS TOOLBAR

A point can be defined by its coordinates from a reference point (origin or selected point), or with respect to an element. You can edit any point by double clicking on it or its identifier in the specification tree. The commands located in the *Points* toolbar, reading left to right, are

- Point: The *Point* command allows you to create a point by entering coordinates relative to the origin or another point. It also allows you to create a point on a curve or surface relative to a point (end point, corner, reference point) on the curve or surface.

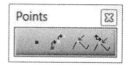

- Points Creation Repetition: The *Points Creation Repetition* command enables you to create several instances of a point.
- Extremum: Creates the extremum point of an element in a given direction.
- Extremum Polar: Creates the extremum point of an element in a given direction in polar coordinates.

THE LINE-AXIS TOOLBAR

Lines can be used as guides, axes, or directions. They can also be joined to other elements. Lines can be created from points or vertices. They can be created on curves or surfaces. Lines have a direction associated with them depending on how you choose your start and end point. You can edit any line by double clicking on it or its identifier in the specification tree. The commands located in the *Line-Axis* toolbar, reading left to right, are

- Line: The *Line* command allows you to create lines in various ways. A few examples are; between two points, from a point extending in a specified direction, and normal to a plane.

- Axis: The *Axis* command creates a reference element that is usually used to indicate symmetry.
- Polyline: The *Polyline* command allows you to create multiple lines that are connected together.

THE PLANES TOOLBAR

Planes are reference elements that aid in the drawing process. Planes can be created from points or lines. They can be created on curves or surfaces. You can edit any plane by double clicking on it or its identifier in the specification tree. The commands located in the *Planes* toolbar, reading left to right, are

- Plane: The *Plane* command allows you to create a reference plane in a variety of ways.

- Points and Planes Repetition: The *Points and Planes Repetition* command creates multiple points and planes along a curve at a specified interval.
- Planes Between: The *Planes Between* command allows you to create any number of planes between two existing planes in one step.

THE PROJECT-COMBINE TOOLBAR

The *Project-Combine* toolbar contains commands that are used to project points, lines and curves onto supporting elements such as a reference plane. The commands, reading from left to right, are

- Projection: Projects a point or curve onto a support element.
- Combine: Creates geometry resulting from the intersection of the extrusion of two elements along two directions.
- Reflect Line: Creates the reflect line on a support along a direction with an angle.
- Silhouette: Creates the silhouette on a support along a direction or from an origin.

THE CURVE OFFSET TOOLBAR

The *Curve Offset* toolbar contains commands that allow you to create offset geometry based on a referenced curved. Similar to the *Offset* command in the *Part Design* workbench. The commands, reading from left to right, are

- Parallel Curve: Creates a curve offset from a referenced curved, on a support surface.
- Rolling Offset: Creates a rolling offset which is an offset curve that travels all the way around the referenced curve and creates an envelope.
- 3D Curve Offset: Creates a curve offset from a referenced curve, a direction and corner parameters.

THE CIRCLE-CONIC TOOLBAR

The *Circle-Conic* toolbar contains commands that are used to create curved elements. The commands, reading from left to right, are

- Circle: Used to create circles. Unlike drawing a circle in the *Sketcher* workbench, a support plane or surface must be specified. If the surface is not flat, the circle will be projected normally onto the surface.
- Corner: This command creates a fillet between two elements.
- Connect Curve: This command creates a curve that will connect two elements.
- Conic: Creates a parabola, hyperbola or ellipse type curves.

THE CURVES TOOLBAR

Curves are used as guides, reference elements, or as limits to surfaces. The commands located in the *Curves* toolbar are used to create complex curves. The commands, reading from left to right, are

- <u>Spline:</u> A spline is a fitted curve that connects several points. Tangencies may be specified at its ends.
- <u>Helix:</u> A helix is a spiral that travels along a specified axis.
- <u>Spiral:</u> Creates a curve in the shape of spirals, that is in 2D plane, as opposed to the helical curves.
- <u>Spine:</u> Creates a spine that is a curve normal to a list of ordered planes or planar curves. These spines are useful when creating complex surfaces such as swept, lofted, or filleted surfaces..
- <u>Isoparametric curve:</u> Creates isoparametric curves on a surface. Because the curve and its supporting surface are associated, any changes to the surface will result in the automatic update of the curve.

TUTORIAL 6.1 START

The part modeled in this tutorial is shown on the right. Reference elements (points, lines, planes, splines, ect...) are used to define surfaces. Once a surface model is created in the *Generative Shape Design* workbench, the part is taken to the *Part Design* workbench and solids are created.

Section 1: Points and lines

1) Enter the **Generative Shape Design** workbench. In the *3D Part / Physical Product* window name your *3D Part* and *Physical Representation* **T61SailBoard.** (Remember: If necessary, place your name before the part name.)

2) Make your **PartBody** the **In Work Object** and set your length units to be **Millimeters** (Tools – Options... – Parameters and Measures)

(Note: If you need to search for a document created in the *Generative Shape Design* workbench, search **3DPart: ***)

3) Insert a point at the origin. Select the **Point** icon. In the *Point Definition* window fill in the following fields:
   - Point type: **Coordinates**
   - X = *0 mm*, Y = *0 mm*, Z = *0 mm*
   - Reference Point: **Default (Origin)**.

4) Create a line that starts at the origin and travels 100 mm in the z direction. Select the **Line** 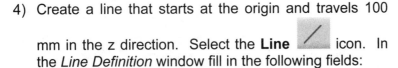 icon. In the *Line Definition* window fill in the following fields:
   - Line type: **Point-Direction**
   - Point: **Point.1** (the point at the origin)
   - Direction: **Z Component** (right click to access the directions)
   - Support: **Default (None)**
   - Start: *0 mm*
   - End: *100 mm*
   - Length type: **Length**.

5) Create a point that is (-10, 30, -50) millimeters away from the top end of the line. Select the **Point** icon. In the *Point Definition* window fill in the following fields:

- `Point type:` Coordinates
- X = *-10 mm*, Y = *30 mm*, Z = *-50 mm*
- `Reference Point:` **Line.1\Vertex** (The point at the top end of the line. This is not the end at the origin.).

6) Create points at (*0, 60, -70*), (*-10, -15, -50*), and (*0, -30, -70*) millimeters away from the same end of the line.

7) Create a line the starts at Point.3 (see figure) and is perpendicular to the Line.1. Select the **Line** icon. In the *Line Definition* window fill in the following fields:

- `Line type:` **Angle/Normal to curve**
- `Curve:` **Line.1**
- `Support:` **yz plane**
- `Point:` **Point.3**
- `Angle:` *90 deg*
- `Start:` *0 mm*
- `End:` *60 mm*
- `Length type:` **Length**
- Use the **Reverse Direction** icon if necessary.

8) Create a similar **Line** that starts at Point.5 (see figure). Use the **Reverse Direction** icon if necessary. (Line length is **30** mm)

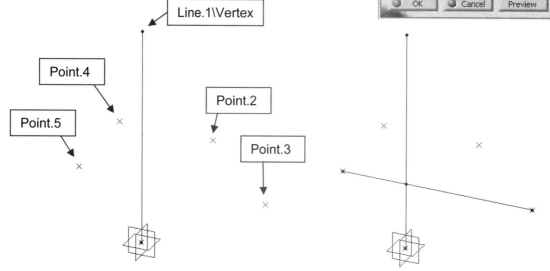

Section 2: Splines

1) Create a **Spline** between **Line.1\Vertex**, **Point.2**, and **Point.3**. (Refer to the figure on the previous page.) Create a similar **Spline** between **Line.1\Vertex**, **Point.4**, and **Point.5**.

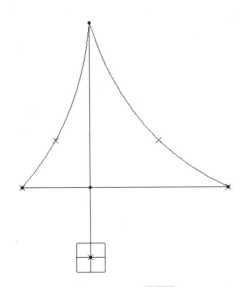

2) Create four **Points** that are located at (*50, -10, 0*), (*-50, -10, 0*), (*0, -10, 15*), and (*0, -10, -15*) millimeters relative to the origin. (Hint: To speed up the entry of the coordinates, use the Tab key to move between fields.)

3) Create a **Spline** using the 4 newly created points. In the *Spline Definition* window make sure to activate the **Close Spline** toggle, only after you have selected all the supporting points, to create a smooth closure.

Don't forget to close the spline.

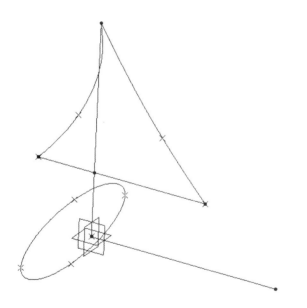

4) Draw a **Line** that starts at the origin and travels **100 mm** in the **y direction**.

5) Create 3 equally spaced point/plane pairs along the newly created line. Select the **Points and Planes Repetition** icon. In the *Points & Planes Repetition Definition* window fill in the following fields:
- First Point: **Point.1** (the point at the origin)
- Curve: **Line.4** (the newly created line)
- Parameters: **Instances**
- Second Point: **Default (Extremity)**
- Activate the **Create normal planes also** toggle.
Select **OK.**

6) **Propagate**.

7) Project the ellipse located near the origin on to each of the newly created planes. Select the **Projection**

icon. In the *Projection Definition* window fill in the following fields:
- Projection type: **Normal**
- Projected: **Spline.3**
- Support: **Plane.1**

Follow a similar procedure for the remaining planes.

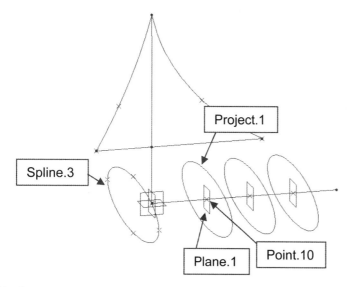

8) Scale the ellipse associated with Plane.1 by 80%.

Select the **Scale** icon. This icon is located in the *Transformations* sub-toolbar which is located in the *Operations* toolbar. In the *Scaling Definition* window fill in the following fields:
- Element: **Projection.1**
- Reference: **Point.10**
- Ratio: *0.8*.

9) Using a similar process, scale the second projection by 60% and the third projection by 40%.

10) Insert points at the top of each of the three scaled ellipses. Select the **Extremum**

    icon located in the *Points* sub-toolbar. In the *Extremum Definition* window fill in the following fields:

- `Element`: Select the first scaled ellipse.
- `Direction`: Right click on this field and select **Z Component**.

Use a similar procedure to place a point on the top of the two remaining scaled ellipses.

11) Create a **Spline** that connects the 5 points indicated in the figure.

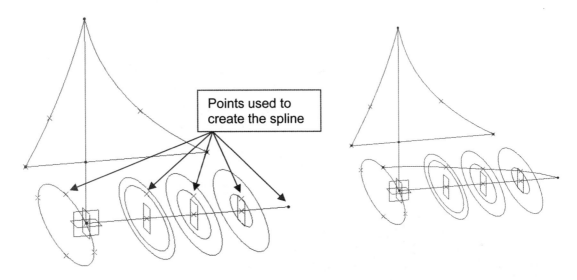

Points used to create the spline

12) Draw a **2mm** radius **Circle** centered at the origin and supported by the **xy plane**. To make a complete circle click on the **whole circle** icon.

13) **Propagate**.

Section 3: Surfaces

1) Create surfaces for the sails. Select the **Fill** icon. This icon is located in the *Surfaces* toolbar. Select **Spline.1, Line.2,** and **Line.1** (see figure). Use a similar procedure to create a surface between **Spline.2, Line.3,** and **Line.1**.

Fill Surface Definition

| Outer Boundaries | Inner Boundaries | | |

No.	Curves	Supports	Continuity
1	Spline.1		
2	Line.2		
3	Line.1		

AddAfter   Replace   Remove
AddBefore   ReplaceSupport   RemoveSupport

Continuity: Tangent

Passing element(s): No selection

☐ Planar Boundary Only

☐ Deviation: 0.001mm

☑ Canonical portion detection

OK   Cancel   Preview

Line.1

Spline.1

Spline.2

Line.3

Line.2

2) Activate the *Graphic Properties* toolbar. At the top pull down menu, select

Graphic Properties — 100% — × — None

View – Toolbars – Graphic Properties. The *Graphic Properties* toolbar may be used to change the color of your surfaces. Try to change the color of your sails.

3) Create a mast by sweeping the circle drawn at the origin along the vertical line. Select the **Sweep** icon. This icon is located in the Surfaces toolbar. In the *Swept Surface Definition* window fill in the following fields:
   - `Profile`: **Circle.1**
   - `Guide curve`: **Line.1**.

4) Use the **Fill** command to fill the top and bottom of the mast with a surface.

5) Use the ellipses and spline to create half of the sail board. Select the **Multisections Surface** icon. Select the 4 ellipses starting with the original ellipse and selecting the other scaled ellipses in order of creation. In the *Multi-sections Surface Definition* window, select the **Spine** tab. Activate the `Spine:` field and select the spline that connects the 4 ellipses.

6) Use the **Fill** command to fill the small open end of the surfboard with a surface.

7) Use the **Plane** command to offset the **zx plane - 10 mm** in the y direction. The plane should be in the same location as the big open end of the surfboard.

8) Mirror the sail board using the newly created plane as the mirroring surface. Select the **Symmetry** icon. This icon is located in the *Transformations* toolbar. In the *Symmetry Definition* window activate the Element: field and select the sail board (**Multi-sections Surface.1**). Activate the Reference: field and select the newly created plane (**Plane.4**).

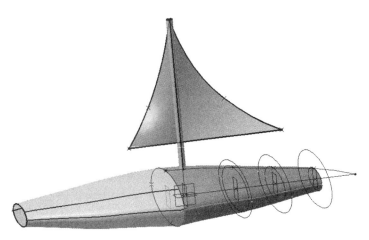

9) Create a point on the top of the mirrored small end of the sail board using the **Extremum** command.

10) Create two **Points** located at (*10, 20,-10*), and (*-10, 20, -10*) millimeters relative to the point at the top-end of the sail board (the last point created).

11) Use the last three points created to define a reference plane. Select the **Plane** icon. In the *Plane Definition* window select the Plane type: to be **Through three points** and then select the three points.

12) Use the newly created plane to create an intersection curve with the mirrored end of the

sail board. Select the **Intersection** icon. In the *Intersection Definition* window select the mirrored end of the surfboard (**Symmetry.1**) as the First Element:, and the newly created plane (**Plane.5**) as the Section Element:.

13) **Propagate**.

14) **Fill** the intersection curve with a surface.

(**PROBLEM?** If the intersection curve does not fill, the most common reason is that the original spline used to create the initial ellipse was not closed. This usually produces a gap at the top of the intersection curve. Access the original ellipse and close it. If you get an error, undo the action and use a *Line* to connect the gap and try to *Fill* it again.)

15) Use the intersection surface to trim off the end

of the surfboard. Select the **Trim** icon. This icon is located in the *Operations* toolbar. In the Trim Definition window select the mirrored end of the surfboard (**Symmetry.1**) as Element 1:, and the intersection surface (**Fill.6**) as Element 2:. (If the *Trim* command is trimming off the wrong side, select the *Other side* button.)

16) If the intersection curve lost its surface, **Fill** it again.

17) Create a point on the surface of the angled end of the sail board (the intersection surface). Select the **Point**

icon. In the *Point Definition* window fill in the following fields:
- `Point type`: **On plane**
- `Plane`: select the angled plane used to create the intersection (Plane.5).
- `H`: *0 mm*
- `V`: *70 mm*
- `Reference Point`: **Default (Origin)**.
- `Projection Surface`: **Default (None)**.

18) Create a line that starts at the newly created point and travels out from the surface 30 mm in a normal

direction. Select the **Line** icon. In the *Line Definition* window fill in the following fields:
- `Line type`: **Normal to surface**
- `Surface`: select the angled end of the surfboard
- `Point`: select the newly created point
- `Start`: *0 mm*
- `End`: *30 mm*
- `Length Type` **Length**.
- You may have to use `Reverse Direction` to get the line to travel away from the surfboard.

19) Create a **Polyline** using the ends of the newly created line and the point indicated in the figure.

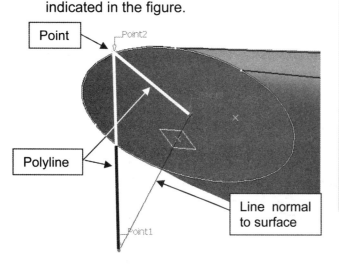

Point

Polyline

Line normal to surface

20) **Fill** 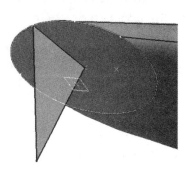 the triangular curve with a surface.

21) **Join** the two halves and the filled end of the sail board.

22) **Propagate**.

Section 4: Creating solids

1) Enter the **Part Design** workbench (**Start - Mechanical - Part Design**).

2) Activate the **Surface-Based Features (Extended)** toolbar if it is not already active.

3) Create a solid using the joined surface used to define the sail board. Select the

Close Surface icon. Select the sail board and click **OK** in the *CloseSurface Definition* window. Notice that the surface of the sail board may now look checkered, but if it doesn't, don't worry. This is because both the solid and the surface now exist in the same space. Go to the specification tree and hide the surface used to define the sail board (Join.1).

4) Use the **Close Surface** command to create a solid out of the swept mast. Then, hide the surface (Sweep.1).

5) We no longer need to see the reference elements (points, lines, planes, etc..). You may hide all of these if you like.

6) Now that you have solid, you may apply any *Part Design* workbench specific command to them. Apply a *1.5 mm* radius **Edge Fillet** to the end of the surfboard that does not have the fin.

7) Play around with other *Part Design* commands to reassure yourself that the Sail Board body is indeed solid.

NOTES:

Chapter 6:
GNERATIVE SURFACE
DESIGN FUNDAMENTALS

Tutorial 6.2: Surfaces toolbar

FEATURED TOPICS & COMMANDS

THE SURFACE TOOLBAR 2

TUTORIAL 6.2 START 3

Section 1: Multisections surface (Loft)...3

Section 2: Extruded surface 5

Section 3: Blended surface...7

Section 4: Spheres and Cylinders 9

Section 5: Revolved surface...11

Section 6: Creating solids...14

PREREQUISITE KNOWLEDGE & COMMANDS

- Entering workbenches
- The *Sketcher* workbench and associated commands
- The *Part Design* workbench and associated commands
- The *Wireframe* toolbar

THE SURFACE TOOLBAR

The commands located in the *Surfaces* toolbar are used to create surfaces that are defined by one or more reference elements. The sub-toolbars / commands, reading from left to right, are

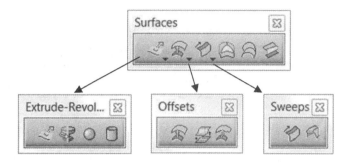

- Extrude-Revolve: The commands located in the Extrude-Revolve toolbar allow you to create surfaces from curves.
    - o Extrude: An extruded surface is created from an open or closed curve. Its direction and limits are specified.
    - o Revolve: A revolved surface is created from an open or closed curve. The axis and angle of rotation are specified.
    - o Sphere: The *Sphere* command allows you to create a complete or incomplete sphere. Limits for the sphere may be specified in both the revolved direction (meridian) and the top to bottom direction (parallel).
    - o Cylinder: The *Cylinder* command allows you to create a complete or incomplete cylinder.
- Offset toolbar: An offset surface is created from an existing surface. An offset distance and direction are specified. The resulting surface is parallel to the existing one.
- Sweeps toolbar: A swept surface is created from an open or closed curve that is swept along guide curves.
- Fill: The filled surface is created between joined curves. The shape of the resulting surface depends on the continuity between the support surfaces (if any) and the fill surface.
- Multisections Surface: A multisections surface or lofted surface is defined by several parameters including; tangency, closing point, coupling, and guide curve.
- Blend: The blend surface is created between two curves. The curves used must be single edge curves and not closed. The shape of the resulting surface depends on the continuity between the support surfaces (if any) and the blend surface.

TUTORIAL 6.2 START

The part modeled in this tutorial is created with reference elements and surfaces. The surfaces are created in a variety of ways in order to gain experience with as many commands in the *Surfaces* toolbar as possible.

Section 1: Multisections surface (Loft)

1) Enter the **Generative Shape Design** workbench. In the *3D Part / Physical Product* window name your *3D Part* and *Physical Representation* **T62Hammer**.

2) Make your **PartBody** the **In Work Object** and set your length units to be **Inches** (Tools – Options... – Parameters and Measures)

3) Create 5 **Points** that are located at (**0.5, 0, 0**), (**-0.5, 0, 0**), (**0, 0, -0.625**), (**0, 0, 0.625**), and (**0, 11, 0**) relative to the **origin**. (Hint: Double clicking on the command keeps it active.)

4) Create 4 **Points** that are located at (**0.3125, 0, 0**), (**-0.3125, 0, 0**), (**0, 0, 0.4375**), (**0, 0, -0.4375**) relative to the **Point.5** (the point located 11 inches from the origin).

5) Use a **Spline** to connect the first 4 points and last 4 points as shown in the figure. Start and end the spline at the top and activate the **Close spline** toggle.

Start and end spline at the top.

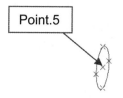

Point.5

6) Create 12 **Points** that are located at (**0, 2, 0.594**), (**0, 4, 0.531**), (**0, 6, 0.5**), (**0, 8, 0.406**), (**0, 9, 0.375**), (**0, 10, 0.344**), (**0.4375, 2, 0**), (**0.406, 4, 0**), (**0.375, 6, 0**), (**0.3125, 8, 0**), (**0.25, 9, 0**), (**0.219, 10, 0**) relative to the **origin**.

7) Use a **Spline** to connect the first 6 points and last 6 points with the points on the two ellipses as shown in the figure.

8) Use a multisections surface to loft together the two ellipses using the two long splines as guides.

Select the **Multisections Surface** icon. In the *Multi-sections Surface* Definition window, activate the *Section* area and select the two ellipse (Spline.1 and Spline.2). Activate the *Guide* area and select the two long splines (Spline.3 and Spline.4). Make sure both closing points are at the top.

9) **Propagate**.

Section 2: Extruded surface

1) Create 4 **Points** that are located at (*0.25, 0.5, 0.375*), (*-0.25, 0.5, 0.375*), (*0.25, 0.5, -0.375*), (*-0.25, 0.5, -0.375*) relative to the **Point.5** (the point located 11 inches from the origin).

2) Draw 4 **Lines** connecting the last 4 points drawn as shown in the figure.

3) Create rounded corners or fillets at each vertex of the rectangle. Select the **Corner** icon located in the *Circle-Conic* sub-toolbar. Select two adjoining lines to be Element 1: and Element 2:. Activate both **Trim element** toggles and enter a Radius: of *0.19 in*. Repeat this procedure for the next two corners. On the last corner you need to activate the **Corner On Vertex** toggle.

4) **Extrude** the cornered rectangle by *1 in* along the **Y Axis**.

5) **Propagate**.

Section 3: Blended surface

1) Create a surface that connects *Multi-sections surface.1* and *Extrude.1*. Select the **Blend** icon. In the *Blend Definition* window, activate the First curve: field and select the spline used to create the end of *Multi-sections surface.1* (**Spline.2**). Activate the Second curve: field and select the cornered rectangle. Note where the *First Point* and *Second Point* lie. They should be across from each other to prevent twist. If your *Second Point* is not across from your *First Point*, click on the **Closing Points** tab and **Replace** your *Second Point* with a point that is across from the *First Point*.

Need to move the *Second Point* to be across from the *First Point*.

The *Second Point* is now across from the *First Point*.

2) Notice that the interface between *Blend.1* and *Extrude.1* is discontinuous or sharp. Make that interface smooth. Get back into the *Blend Definition* window by double clicking on **Blend.1** in your specification tree. Activate the *Second support* field and select **Extrude.1**. (A gap WARNING window may appear. Just click OK.)

3) **Fill** the two ends of the handle.

4) **Join** all surfaces of the handle.

Section 4: Spheres and Cylinders

1) Insert a new body (**Insert – Body**).

2) Insert a new **Plane** that is offset from the **zx plane** by **11.75 in**.

3) Insert a **Point** at (**0, 11.75, 0**) inches relative to the origin. Then insert a **Point** at (**0, 0, -1**) inches relative to the previous point.

4) Locate the Extrude-Revolve sub-toolbar.

5) Select the **Cylinder** icon. In the *Cylinder Surface Definition* window fill in the following fields;
   - Point: **Point.27** (most recently created point)
   - Direction: **Z** Component
   - Radius: *0.5 in*
   - Length 1: *0 in*
   - Length 2: *0.875 in*.

6) Insert a **Point** at (*0, 0, 1*) inches relative to the point in the middle of the offset plane (Point.26).

Point.26

7) Select the **Sphere** icon. In the *Sphere Surface Definition* window, fill in the following fields;
   - Center: **Point.28** (most recently created point)
   - Sphere radius: *0.438 in*
   - Select the incomplete sphere icon
   - Parallel Start Angle: *0 deg*
   - Parallel End Angle: *90 deg*
   - Meridian Start Angle: *0 deg*
   - Meridian End Angle: *360 deg*.

8) **Fill** the bottom of the cylinder. The end that is furthest away from the handle.

9) **Propagate**.

Section 5: Revolved surface

1) Insert 2 **Points** at (*-0.5, 0, 0*) and (*-0.44, 0, 0.25*) inches relative to the center point of the cylinder (Point.27).

2) Insert 2 **Points** at (*-0.438, 0, 0*) and (*-0.25, 0, -0.25*) inches relative to the center point of the sphere (Point.28).

3) Insert a **Point** at (*-0.5, 0, 0*) inches relative to the point located in the middle of the offset plane (Point.26).

4) Create a **Spline** connecting the last 5 points created as shown in the figure.

5) Create a **Line** that connects the center of the cylinder with the center of the sphere.

6) **Revolve** the spline *360 deg* about the line.

7) Create an **Intersection** curve between the revolved surface and the handle. When you select the **OK** button a *Multi-Result Management* window will appear. This means that two intersections were created and we need to tell CATIA which one to keep. After you select the **OK** button, a *Near Definition* window will appear. CATIA wants you to choose an element that is near the intersection curve that you want to keep. Select an edge of the handle end.

Select an edge near the intersection to keep.

8) Hide the handle. Right click on **PartBody** and select **Hide/Show**.

9) **Extrude** the intersection curve (**Near.1**) *1 inch* in both directions along the **Y Axis / Component**.

10) **Trim** **Revolute.1** and **Extrude.2** to create a hole going through the hammer head. Select the **Other side / previous elements** buttons until the desired result is obtained.

11) **Join** all the surfaces of the hammer head.

12) **Show** the hammer handle and hide all reference elements.

13) **Propagate**.

Section 6: Creating solids

1) Enter the **Part Design** ⚙ workbench.

2) Right click on **PartBody** and select **Define in Work Object**.

3) Use the **Close Surface** command to create a solid out of the handle (Join.1).

4) Hide the surfaces of the handle (Join.1).

5) Apply a *0.06 in* x *45 deg* **Chamfer** to the end of the hammer handle. The end away from the hammer head.

Chamfer Definition	? X
Mode:	Length1/Angle
Length 1:	0.06in
Angle:	45deg
Object(s) to chamfer:	1 Edge
Propagation:	Tangency
☐ Reverse	
● OK	● Cancel Preview

6) Right click on **Body.2** and select **Define in Work Object**.

7) Use the **Close Surface** command to create solids out of the hammer head (Join.2).

8) Hide the surfaces of the hammer head (Join.2).

9) Apply a *0.06 in* radius **Fillet** to the striking surface of the hammer head and the edge of the ball, as shown in the figure.

10) Make the handle **Wood** and the hammer head **Steel**.

NOTES:

NOTES:

Chapter 6: GENERATIVE SURFACE DESIGN FUNDAMENTALS

Tutorial 6.3: Operations toolbar

FEATURED TOPICS & COMMANDS

THE OPERATIONS TOOLBAR 2

THE JOIN-HEALING TOOLBAR 2

THE TRIM-SPLIT TOOLBAR 3

THE EXTRACTS TOOLBAR 3

THE FILLETS TOOLBAR...3

THE TRANSFORMATIONS TOOLBAR...4

THE EXTRAPOLATE TOOLBAR 4

THE GRID TOOLBAR 4

TUTORIAL 6.3 START 5

    Section 1: Using Supports 5

    Section 2: Split, Trim, and Extrapolate 9

    Section 3: Extracting..12

PREREQUISITE KNOWLEDGE & COMMANDS

- Entering workbenches
- The *Sketcher* workbench and associated commands
- The *Part Design* workbench and associated commands
- The *Wireframe* and *Surfaces* toolbars

THE OPERATIONS TOOLBAR

The *Operations* toolbar contains commands the will help you transform and modify surfaces and curves and make it easier to produce the desired shape. The commands and sub-toolbars located in the *Operations* toolbar, reading left to right, are

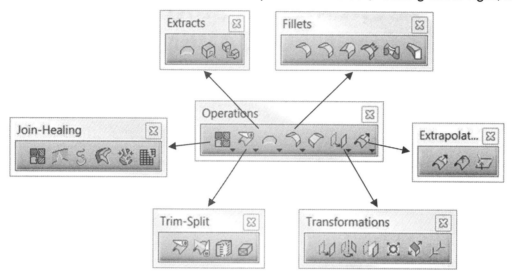

- <u>Join-Healing toolbar:</u> Contains commands that will join, fill gaps, restore, and disassemble adjoining elements.
- <u>Trim-Split toolbar:</u> Contains commands that will cut one side of intersecting elements.
- <u>Extracts toolbar:</u> Contains commands that create curves and surfaces from surface boundaries and edges.
- <u>Fillets toolbar:</u> Contains commands to make various types of fillets.
- <u>Transformations toolbar:</u> Contains commands that will transform the size, position, orientation, etc... of an element.
- <u>Extrapolate:</u> The *Extrapolate* command extends one element to the boundary of another.

THE JOIN-HEALING TOOLBAR

The commands contained in the *Join-Healing* toolbar, reading left to right, are

- <u>Join:</u> The *Join* command allows you to join one or more adjacent elements into a single element. Multiple curves or surfaces may be joined. You can define a *Merge distance* and an *Angle tolerance*. The *Merge distance* is the maximum gap distance under which the two elements can be joined. The *Angle tolerance* specifies the maximum interface angle under which the two elements can be joined.
- <u>Healing:</u> The *Healing* command fills in gaps between two elements. A *Merge distance* or maximum gap that will be filled, and a *Distance objective* or minimum gap that will be filled, may be specified.
- <u>Curve Smooth:</u> Smoothes tangency and curvature discontinuities of a curve under given thresholds.

- Surface Simplification: Simplifies the topology of a surface under given thresholds.
- Untrim: The *Untrim* command allows you to rebuild an element that has been split one or more times.
- Disassemble: The *Disassemble* command breaks a multi-celled surface or curve into its individual cells.

THE TRIM-SPLIT TOOLBAR

The commands contained in the *Split-Trim* toolbar, reading left to right, are

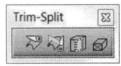

- Split: The *Split* command cuts or splits one element using a cutting element. One side of the element is cut.
- Trim: The *Trim* command cuts or trims two intersecting elements. One side of each element is cut.
- Sew Surface: Sews or connects a surface to an object.
- Remove Face: Removes one or more faces.

THE EXTRACTS TOOLBAR

The commands contained in the *Extracts* toolbar, reading left to right, are

- Boundary: The *Boundary* command creates a curve from a surface boundary. Limits may or may not be set.
- Extract: The *Extract* command creates a curve from a surface edge. It can also be used to extract a surface. Limits may not be set.
- Multiple Extract: Extracts a group of elements.

THE FILLETS TOOLBAR

The commands contained in the Fillets toolbar, reading left to right, are

- Shape Fillet: Creates a fillet between two surfaces.
- Edge Fillet: Creates a fillet on a surface's edge.
- Variable Fillet: Creates a fillet whose radius varies at each specified points.
- Chordal Fillet: Creates a fillet on a surface's edge. The fillets width at various point may be specified.
- Face-Face Fillet: Creates a fillet between two non-intersection faces.
- Tritangent Fillet: Creates a tritangent fillet from three faces you specify, by removing one of the three faces. The fillet surface is obtained by rolling a sphere, whose radius is automatically computed to be tangent to the three surfaces and then removes one surface.

THE TRANSFORMATIONS TOOLBAR

The commands contained in the *Transformations* toolbar, reading left to right, are

- Translate: The *Translate* command makes a duplicate element that is a specified distance away from the original. Multiple duplicates may be created using the repeat option.
- Rotate: The *Rotate* command makes a duplicate element that is rotated about an axis by a specified angle. Multiple duplicates may be created using the repeat option.
- Symmetry: The *Symmetry* command mirrors an element about a reference element.
- Scaling: The *Scaling* command makes a duplicate element that is of a different size from the original. Multiple duplicates may be created using the repeat option.
- Affinity: The *Affinity* command creates a scaled version of an element. However, the scale factors in each direction may be different.
- Axis to Axis: The *Axis to Axis* command takes an element that is supported by one axis and creates a duplicate that is supported by another axis.

THE EXTRAPOLATE TOOLBAR

The commands contained in the *Extrapolate* toolbar, reading left to right, are

- Extrapolate: Creates a surface by extrapolation of one of its boundaries, or a curve at one of its endpoints.
- Invert Orientation: Inverts an element's orientation.
- Near: Creates, from the multi-element, the element nearest or farthest to the reference element.

THE GRID TOOLBAR

The *Grid* toolbar is located in the *Tools* toolbar. The commands located in the *Grid* toolbar, reading left to right, are

- Work on Support: This command allows you to work on a sketch plane.
- Work on Support 3D: Allows working on a set of three support planes.
- Snap to Point: This command allows you to snap to the grid points.
- Working Supports Activity: This command exits the working support mode.
- Grid Featurization Switch: Creates either featurized lines or featurized planes on the grid lines.

- <u>Plane System:</u> Provides tools that let you define a number of planes in a given direction.

TUTORIAL 6.3 START

The part modeled in this tutorial is a combination of shapes used to illustrate the commands found in the *Operations* toolbar. The reference elements used to constructed the base where drawn using the *Work on Support* command. Several commands found in the *Operations* toolbar and its sub-toolbars are used to modify and add to the base.

<u>Section 1:</u> Using Supports

1) Enter the **Generative Shape Design** workbench. In the *3D Part / Physical Product* window name your *3D Part* and *Physical Representation* **T63SheetMetal.**

2) Make your **PartBody** the **In Work Object** and set your length units to be **Millimeters** (<u>T</u>ools – <u>O</u>ptions... – Parameters and Measures)

3) Pull out the **Grid** toolbar . This sub-toolbar is located in the *Tools* toolbar.

4) Select the **Work on Support** icon. In the first *Work on Support* window select the **zx plane** as the Support:. In the second *Work on Support* window set the Primary spacing: to be ***100 mm*** and the Graduations: to be **10**.

5) Activate the **Snap to point** icon.

6) Draw the following profile using the **Polyline** command.

7) Select the **Works Support Activity** icon to deactivate the support.

Then, select the **Isometric View** icon.

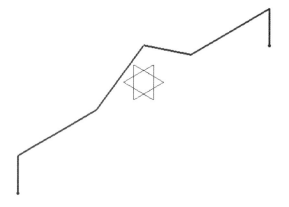

8) **Extrude** the polyline **75 mm** in the positive and negative **y** directions.
(Direction: Y Component)

9) Use the **Work on Support** command to sketch on the **xy plane** with the same grid spacing as before.

10) Hide Extrude.1.

11) Draw the following 2 **Splines** using the points indicated in the figure.

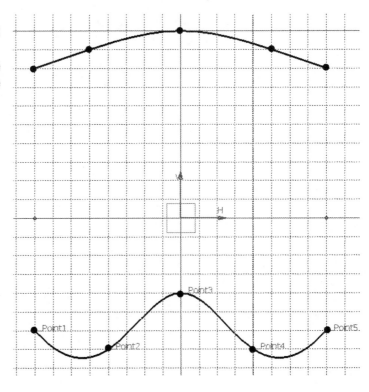

12) Unhide Extrude.1.

13) Select the **Works Support Activity** icon to deactivate the support. Then, select the **Isometric View** icon.

14) **Extrude** each spline **20 mm** in the both the negative and positive **z** directions.

15) **Propagate**.

Section 2: Split, Trim, and Extrapolate

1) Select the **Split** icon. In the *Split Definition* window, activate the `Element to cut:` field and select **Extrude.1**. Activate the `Cutting elements` area and select the extrude created with the wavy spline. Use the **Other side** button if necessary to get the desired results. Notice that the cutting element does not change.

2) Delete Split.1 and select the **Trim** icon. Select Extrude.1 and Extrude.3 (the wave spline extrude). Use the **Other side/ previous elements** buttons if necessary. Notice that both elements get cut.

3) Create a boundary to use in the *Extrapolate* command. (Note: The figure shows Extrude.2 hidden) Select the **Boundary** icon. In the *Boundary Definition* window, fill in the following fields;

- Propagation type: **Point continuity**
- Surface edge: select the original extrude now called **Trim.1**
- Limit 1: select **Point 1** as shown on the figure
- Limit 2: select **Point 2**
- We want the boundary to cover the original polyline shape, if it does not, click on the arrow attached to Point 1.

4) Select the **Extrapolate** icon. In the *Extrapolate Definition* window, fill in the following fields;
- Boundary: **Boundary.1**
- Extrapolate: **Trim.1**
- Type: **Up to element**
- Up to: select the extrude created from the curved spline.

5) Use the **Split** command to achieve the results shown in the figure.

6) **Propagate**.

Section 3: Extracting

1) Select the **Extract** icon , in the *Extracts* sub-toolbar, and select the face indicated in the figure.

Select this face.

Extract Definition

Propagation type: No propagation

Element(s) to extract Extrapol.1\Face.1

Support : No selection

☐ Complementary mode

☐ Federation

Show parameters >>

OK   Cancel   Preview

2) Select the **Extract** icon repeatedly and select the edges indicated in the figure.

Select these edges one at a time.

3) Use the **Boundary** command to extract the remaining edge. You need to select the surface and then use limits to modify the boundary edge. You may have to hide the spline.

Use *Boundary* to extract this edge.

4) **Join** all the edges created in the previous 2 steps.

5) **Extrude** **Extract.1** and **Join.1** individually *40 mm* in the positive **z** direction only.

6) Disassemble the closed extrude so that one of its surfaces can be extruded. Select the closed extrude (Extrude.4 or Extrude.5 depending on the order in which you extruded) then select the **Disassemble** icon, located in the *Join-Healing* sub-toolbar. A *Disassemble* window will appear showing how many elements the extrude will be broken up into. Select **OK**.

7) **Extrude** the back surface of the disassemble extrude **75 mm** in the **y** direction as shown in the figure. (**Problem?** If you get an error, select the surface in the specification tree.)

8) Use the Affinity command to create a scaled duplicate of the open extrude. Select the **Affinity**

 icon, located in the *Transformations* sub-toolbar. In the *Affinity Definition* window, fill in the following fields;

- `Element:` select the open extrude (Extrude.4 or Extrude.5)
- `Origin:` select the point indicated in the figure
- `X: 0.5`, `Y: -1.5`, `Z: 0.5`.

Chapter 6: Exercises

Exercise 6.1: This exercise can be performed after completing the tutorials presented in chapter 6. Model the following parts.

    a) A pair of pliers
    b) A screwdriver
    c) A popup tent
    d) An airplane body
    e) A car body

NOTES:

Chapter 7: IMAGINE AND SHAPE BASICS

INTRODUCTION

Chapter 7 focuses on CATIA's *Imagine and Shape* workbench. The reader will learn how to create basic surfaces and use them to create solids.

The toolbars and commands contained in the following pages will probably not make much sense until you have experienced the Imagine and Shape workbench. After you have created a few shapes, take a second look at the commands and they will start to make more sense. This particular workbench is truly a learn by doing workbench.

TUTORIALS CONTAINED IN CHAPTER 7

- Tutorial 7.1: Car Body
- Tutorial 7.2: Turbine Blade
- Tutorial 7.3: Tea Pot

TOOLBARS & COMMANDS COVERED IN CHAPTER 7

THE IMAGINE AND SHAPE WORKBENCH 2

THE CREATION TOOLBAR 2

    Primitives Tools Palettes 4

    Curves Tools Palettes 5

STYLING SURFACES TOOLBAR 5

MODIFICATION TOOLBAR 6

OPERATIONS TOOLBAR 6

THE IMAGINE AND SHAPE WORKBENCH

The *Imagine and Shape* workbench is used to create complex surfaces. It is a place where creativity supersedes precision. The *Imagine and Shape* workbench contains the following standard workbench specific toolbars.

- Creation toolbar: The commands located in the *Creation* toolbar are used to create 2D and 3D surface elements.

- Styling Surfaces toolbar: The commands located in the *Styling Surfaces* toolbar are used to modify existing elements.

- Modification toolbar: The commands located in the *Modification* toolbar are used to modify the shape of a mesh through various means.

- Operations toolbar: The commands located in the *Operations* toolbar are used to modify or add to an exiting surface.

THE CREATION TOOLBAR

Many of the commands located in the *Creation* toolbar have a *Tools Palette* associated with them. One *Tools Palette* before you create the element and another after the element has been created and is ready to be modified. The *Tools Palette* allows you to choose different options and is command specific. Along with a description of the command, below, a description of the *Tools Palette* options are given. Commands / toolbars located in the *Creation* toolbar, reading left to right, are

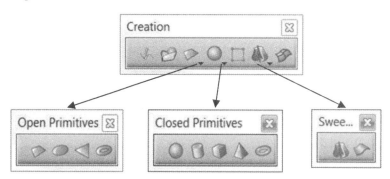

- Sketch Curve: Allows you to sketch a styling curve. *Styling curves* are used as a guide in creating surfaces through commands such as *Sweep*, *Extrude* and *Net Surface*. The commands in the associated *Tools Palette*, reading left to right, are

  - Sketch: Creates a curve lying on the current view plane.
  - Plane Selection: Allows you to sketch a curve lying on an existing plane. You need to select the plane first.
  - Characteristics: Allows you to define the curve characteristics.

- Import Subdivision: Imports a subdivision surface from an OBJ file.
- Open Primitives sub-toolbar: Commands located in the *Open Primitives* toolbar allow you to create two-dimensional surfaces such as *Rectangles*, *Circles*, *Triangles* and *Rings*.
- Closed Primitives: Commands located in the *Closed Primitives* toolbar allow you to create three-dimensional surfaces such as a *Sphere*, *Cylinder*, *Box*, *Pyramid* and *Torus*.
- Number Sections: Defines the number of sections for primitive creation (4 or 8).
- Sweep Primitives: Commands located in the *Sweep Primitives* toolbar allow you to create swept surfaces by revolving or extruding a curve. The commands in the associated *Tools Palette*, reading left to right, are

  - Drawing view: Reframes on the drawing view.
  - Plane Selection: Allows you to select a new plane of drawing.
  - Add Point: Adds points to the curve being created.
  - Move Point: Allows you to move a point.
  - Align Point: Vertically aligns two or more points.
  - Attraction: Adds weight to the points and attracts them to the defining mesh.
  - Erase Point: Allows you to erase a point.
  - Pick a Point: Pick a point.
  - Close Curve: Closes the curve being drawn.
  - Fill Side: Fills the top, bottom or both ends of an open surface.
  - Apply: Applies the modifications.

- Net Surface: Creates a subdivided surface using a net of curves. The commands in the associated *Tools Palette*, reading left to right, are

  - Guide selection: The guide curve defines the direction the surface will be swept.
  - Profiles selection: The profile curve defines the basic shape of the surface.
  - Apply: Applies the modification.

Primitives Tools Palettes

This *Tools Palette* is used to modify *Open*, *Closed*, and *Sweep Primitives*. There are three types of elements that can be selected and manipulated. These include a *Face*, an *Edge* and a *Vertex*. The commands located in this *Tools Palette*, reading left to right, are

- <u>Manage the compass:</u> You can use and manage the compass when modifying a surface. The first command allows you to modify the origin and orientation of the compass. The second command allows you to reset the compass orientation to the model axis.

- <u>Translate:</u> This option allows you to translate an element.

- <u>Local normals:</u> This option allows you to translate vertices along their normal, as if performing a local offset.

- <u>Translate along mesh lines:</u> This option allows you to translate vertices along the edges of the base mesh (mesh lines).

- <u>Rotation:</u> This option allows you to rotate an element.

- <u>Affinity:</u> This option allows you to scale a surface along one or more axes.

- <u>Alignment:</u> This option allows you to align vertices of a mesh by projecting them onto a plane, axis or curve.

- <u>Attraction:</u> This option allows you to adjust the weight applied to edges or vertices in order to attract the surface by the mesh.

- <u>Pick:</u> This option allows you to pick multiple elements of different types.

- <u>Edition:</u> This option allows you to impose numerical values to the modifications.

- <u>Attenuation:</u> This option allows you to set the attenuation for the manipulator's displacement

- <u>Select elements:</u> The first selection mode allows you to select any type of element. The second selection mode allows you to select only *Faces*. The third selection mode allows you to select only *Edges*. The forth selection mode allows you to only select *Vertices*. The last select mode allows you to select all of the same kind of element. For example, if you select an edge, all edges will be selected.

Curves Tools Palettes

The commands located in this *Tools Palette*, reading left to right, are

- Sketch: Creates or modifies a curve or a part of the curve by sketching.

- Manipulation: Modifies the curve or a part of the curve by direct manipulation.

- Smooth: Smoothes the curve or a part of the curve.

- Local tuning: Tunes the curve or a part of the curve using the manipulators.

- Erasing: Erases some part of the curve.

- Planarity: Keeps the curve planar.

- Characteristics: Defines the geometrical characteristics of the curve such as order and the number of arcs.

- Area selection: Activates the area selection to restrict the manipulation.

- Transformations: Activates the transformation mode enabling translation, rotation and scaling operations.

STYLING SURFACES TOOLBAR

The commands in the *Styling Surfaces* Toolbar, reading left to right, are

- Mesh Tools: Mutli-tools utilities to modify the mesh.
- Merge: Merges several meshes.
- Extrusion: Extrudes one or more faces or edges simultaneously.
- Face Cutting: Cuts a face into sections in a specified direction. The commands in the associated *Tools Palette*, reading left to right, are

  o Cut multi-edges: Inserts one or more sections on a face.
  o Cut manipulation: Allows you to manipulate the location of a section edge.
  o Section Number Edition: Allows you to define the number of sections using a dialog box.
  o Apply: Applies the modification.

- Face Subdivision: Subdivides one or more faces.
- Erasing: Removes the selected faces or edges.
- Cut by Plane: Cuts subdivision with a plane.

MODIFICATION TOOLBAR

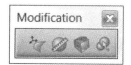

The commands in the *Modification* Toolbar, reading left to right, are

- Modification: Modifies the selected shape using various methods.
- Dimension: Shows a shape's dimensions and allows you to set their value.
- Draft of subdivision: Applies a draft angle to a subdivision.
- Multi-Selection: Manages the current activated features.

OPERATIONS TOOLBAR

The commands in the *Operations* Toolbar, reading left to right, are

- Link: Links some vertices of a subdivision surface to a point, a curve, or another subdivision surface.
- Symmetry: Mirrors a subdivision surface by a plane.
- Working Zone Definition: Allows you to define the vertices that will be visible in all commands.
- View and Selection Mode: Defines view and selection mode for hidden faces of each subdivision.

Chapter 7:
IMAGINE AND SHAPE BASICS

Tutorial 7.1: Car Body

FEATURED TOPICS & COMMANDS

TUTORIAL 7.1 START 2

   Section 1: Basic Shape 2

   Section 2: Erasing 6

   Section 3: Final touches 6

   Section 4: Part Design 8

PREREQUISITE KNOWLEDGE & COMMANDS

- Entering workbenches
- The *Generative Shape Design* workbench and associated commands
- The *Part Design* workbench and associated commands

TUTORIAL 7.1 START

The part modeled in this tutorial is shown on the right. The objective of this tutorial is to familiarize the reader with some basic *Image and Shape* commands. The car body is more of an artistic rendering rather than conforming to exact dimensions. Therefore, each person completing this tutorial will most likely have a slightly different version of the car body.

Section 1: Basic Shape

1) Enter the **Imagine and Shape** workbench. In the *3D Part / Physical Product* window name your *3D Part* and *Physical Representation* **T71Car.** (Remember: If necessary, place your name before the part name.)

2) Make your **PartBody** the **In Work Object** and set your length units to be **Millimeters** (Tools – Options... – Parameters and Measures)

(Note: If you need to search for a document created in the *Imagine and Shape* workbench, search **3DPart: ***)

3) Pull out the *Quick view* toolbar. We will be using these commands very frequently throughout this tutorial.

4) Select the **zx plane** and then insert a **Sphere**

with **4 Sections** . These commands are located in the *Creation* toolbar. Notice that once the Sphere is inserted, a Tools Palette appears. The commands located in the Tools Palette will allows us to modify the shape of the sphere.

5) Activate the **Translate** and **Face** options in the *Tools Palette*. Select the right face of the mesh (the box that surrounds the sphere). Notice that the a compass attaches itself to the selected face. Pull on the **Y'**, **Z'**, **X'** axes and the **pie shape** in turn and notice the effect. **Undo** any modifications that you have performed to get the sphere back to its original size.

6) Select the right face of the mesh and then pull on the **Y'** axis and watch the displacement value. Pull until this number reaches approximately **250** mm. (Note: The displacement value resets every time you release the mouse.)

7) Select the front face of the mesh and pull the **X'** axis approximately **100** mm.

8) Click on the **Select** icon. This will exit the modification mode.

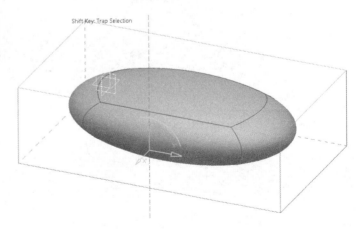

9) Select the **Face Cutting** 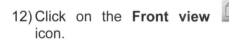 icon, select the shape and then select a mesh edge traveling in the **y** direction. Put the *Face Cutting* slider up to **9** sections

   and then select **Apply** in the *Tools Palette*.

10) Click on the **Modifications** icon. (Note: You can also enter the *Modification* mode by double clicking on the shape.)

11) Click off the shape to deselect all elements.

12) Click on the **Front view** icon.

Selection window (hold `Shift` key)

13) Activate the **Edge** option in the *Tools Palette*. We will be **Translating** the top edges in the **z** direction to obtain the following shape. To select the top edges in this view, hold the `shift` key down and draw a window around the edge.

14) Click on the **Isometric view** icon.

15) Select the **Face Cutting** icon, and add **8** sections in the **x** direction. Remember to select **Apply** to accept the modification.

16) Re-enter the **Modification** mode and deselect all.

17) Select all the **Edges** running front to back as indicated in the figure.
To multiple select, hold the Ctrl key down.

Select these edges.

18) Click on the **Right side view** icon.

19) **Translate** the *Edges* in the **z** direction to match the shape shown.

20) Click on the **Isometric view** icon.

21) **Propagate**.

Section 2: Erasing

1) Click on the **Bottom view** icon.

2) Select the **Erasing** icon located in the *Styling Surfaces* toolbar. Select the shape if not already selected. Holding the Ctrl key click on all the bottom faces to erase them. **Apply** the modification when done.

3) Click on the **Front view** icon.

4) Select the **Face Cutting** icon, and add **5** sections in the **z** direction. Select **Apply** to accept the modification.

5) Click on the **Isometric view** icon.

6) **Erasing** the faces shown (both sides and top). **Apply** the modification when done.

7) **Propagate**.

Section 3: Final touches

1) Select the **xy plane** and then add a **Rectangle** .

2) Click on the **Top view** icon.

3) **Translate** the *Rectangle* along the **X'** and **Y'** directions to match the figure. You will need to use both **Face** and **Edge** selection modes.

4) Click on the **Front view** icon.

5) **Translate** the *Rectangle* along the **Z'** to match the figure. You will need to use the **Face** selection modes.

6) Click on the **Isometric view** icon.

7) Add **3 Face Cutting** sections, to the *Rectangle* in both the **x** and **y** directions. Select **Apply** to accept the modification.

8) **Translate** the 4 center faces of the *Rectangle* along the **Z'** about half the height of the car. You may want to use the **Front view** to get a better line of sight.

9) Click on the **Top view** icon.

10) Make sure that the Rectangle intersects the car body at all point. If not, you will have to *Translate* the outside *Edges* to achieve the intersection.

11) Use the **Trim** command, located in the *Shape Operations* toolbar, to achieve the following effect.

12) Click on the **Bottom view** icon.

13) Enter the **Modification** mode and select **Trim.1**.

14) Activate the **Edge** selection mode

and the **Affinity** icon. select all the bottom edges. Once all the bottom edges are selected, hold the Ctrl key down and pull on of the compass axes towards the center of the car body to achieve a rounding effect.

15) **Propagate**.

Section 4: Part Design

1) Enter the *Part Design* workbench (**Start - Mechanical - Part Design**)

2) Add thickness to the car body. Select **Trim.1** in the specification tree and then the **Thick Surface** icon located in the *Surface Based Features* toolbar. Add **3** mm of thickness.

ThickSurface Definition

First Offset: 3mm

Second Offset: 0mm

Object to offset: Trim.1

Reverse Direction

More>>

OK   Cancel   Preview

3) **Hide** *Trim.1*.

4) Use the *Graphic Properties* toolbar to color the car body. Use the Ctrl key to multiple select.

(**Problem?** If you are trying to color one area of the car and the whole car changes color. You have selected an edge.)

Chapter 7: IMAGINE AND SHAPE BASICS

Tutorial 7.2: Turbine Blade

FEATURED TOPICS & COMMANDS

TUTORIAL 7.2 START 2

Section 1: Basic Shape 2

Section 2: Creating sections and shaping 4

PREREQUISITE KNOWLEDGE & COMMANDS

- Entering workbenches
- The *Generative Shape Design* workbench and associated commands
- The *Part Design* workbench and associated commands

TUTORIAL 7.2 START

The part modeled in this tutorial is shown below. The objective of this tutorial is to familiarize the reader with some basic *Image and Shape* commands. To model the *Wind Turbine Blade* we will be using exact dimension along with some artistic shaping.

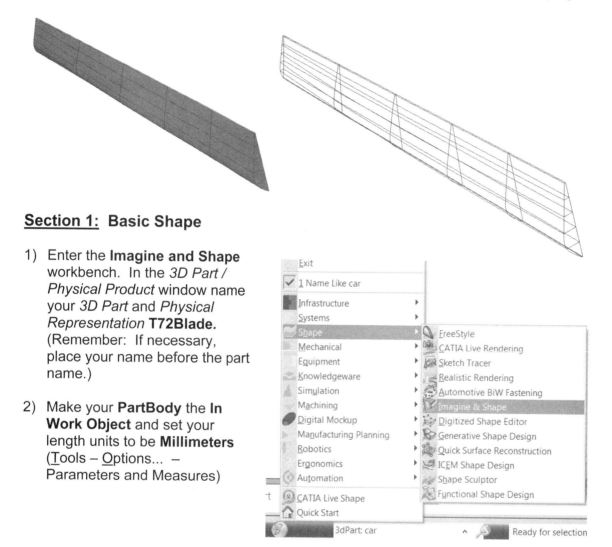

Section 1: Basic Shape

1) Enter the **Imagine and Shape** workbench. In the *3D Part / Physical Product* window name your *3D Part* and *Physical Representation* **T72Blade.** (Remember: If necessary, place your name before the part name.)

2) Make your **PartBody** the **In Work Object** and set your length units to be **Millimeters** (Tools – Options... – Parameters and Measures)

3) Select the **xy plane** and then insert a **Box** with **4 Sections** .

4) Click on the **Dimension** icon. This will give you the size of your box. Note these dimension.

5) Modify the dimensions to produce a **700 x 168 x 44.5** mm *Box*. To modify the dimensions individually, you need to select the **Half Axis Deformation Mode**. Set one of the dimensions to **0** and the other to the intended length. You will have to rotate the part to access the other dimensions.

6) **Translate** the **Vertices** shown in the direction indicated to obtain the following.

7) Click on the **Front view** icon.

8) **Translate** the left top **Edge** by 84 mm. To do this accurately, select the *Edge* and then select the **Editions** icon. Enter a value of **84** in the **z** field.

9) **Propagate**.

Section 2: Creating sections and shaping

1) Click on the **Isometric view** icon.

2) Select the **Face Cutting** icon, and create **4** sections in both the **y** and **z** directions. Select **Apply** in the *Tools Palette*.

3) **Translate** the **Vertex** indicated in the figure to obtain the desired result.

4) Rotate the Blade so that you can see the other end. **Translate** the **Vertices** to obtain the result shown.

5) Adjust the sections in between to obtain a smooth transition.

(Note: If you are building a *Blade* to specific dimensions, you can always using the *Edition* command.)

NOTES:

NOTES:

Chapter 7:
IMAGINE AND SHAPE BASICS

Tutorial 7.3: Tea Pot

FEATURED TOPICS & COMMANDS

TUTORIAL 7.3 START 2

Section 1: Sweep..2

Section 2: Subdivisions and Extrusions..3

Section 3: Lid...5

PREREQUISITE KNOWLEDGE & COMMANDS

- Entering workbenches
- The *Generative Shape Design* workbench and associated commands
- The *Part Design* workbench and associated commands

TUTORIAL 7.3 START

The part modeled in this tutorial on the right. The objective of this tutorial is to familiarize the reader with some basic *Image and Shape* commands. To model the *Tea Pot* we will be using swept surfaces.

Section 1: Sweep

1) Enter the **Imagine and Shape** workbench. In the *3D Part / Physical Product* window name your *3D Part* and *Physical Representation* **T73TeaPot.**

2) Make your **PartBody** the **In Work Object** and set your length units to be **Millimeters** (Tools – Options... – Parameters and Measures)

3) Select the **yz plane** and then select the **Sweep** 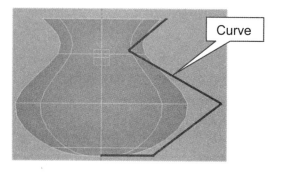 command. Draw a curve similar to the one shown. Use the **Move Point** option to move the vertices if necessary.

4) Rotate the shape so that you can see the bottom of the *Tea Pot*. Select the **Face** and **Attraction** options. Select all the bottom faces as shown and set the *Attraction* to **100%**. (Remember: Use the Ctrl key to multiple select.)

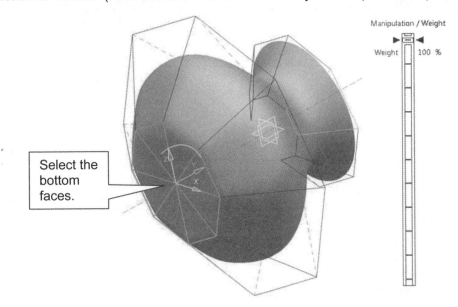

5) **Propagate**.

Section 2: Subdivisions and Extrusions

1) Click on the **Isometric view** icon.

2) Apply a *Face Subdivision* to the face indicated. Select the **Face Subdivision** command and activate the **Face** selection mode. Select the face indicated. Use a *Face Subdivision Ratio* of around **0.5**. **Apply** the modification.

3) **Extrude** 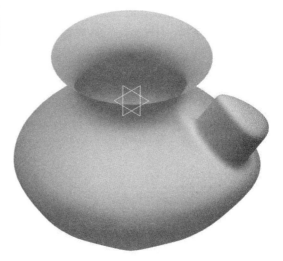 the center face of the newly

   subdivided face 4 times. **Apply**
   between extrusions.

4) **Erase** the end of the spout and then

   Translate the **Vertices** to obtain
   the following result. (Hint: You will most
   likely have to *Translate* the vertices using
   the pie shaped portion of the compass,
   because the axes do not line up.)

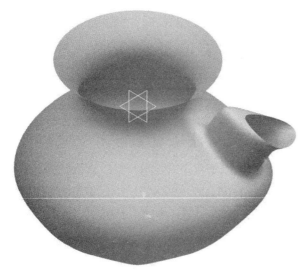

5) Rotate the shape so that you the spout is pointing away from you and you can see
   the back of the *Tea Pot*.

6) Apply a **Face Subdivision** 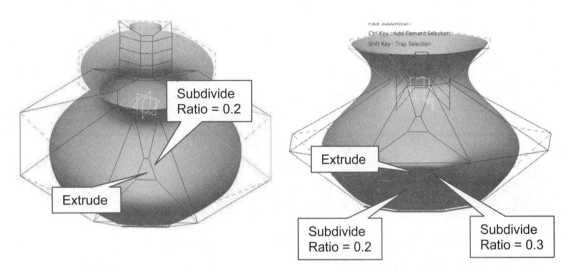 of ratio **0.2** to the two back **Faces** . Apply another **Face Subdivision** of ratio **0.3** to the upper *Face* of the bottom subdivision.

Apply between subdivisions.

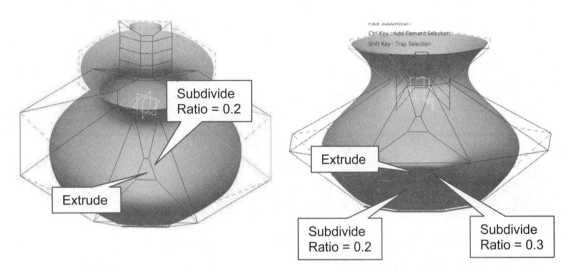

7) **Extrude** the center face of the top subdivided surface 6 times. **Extrude** the face of the bottom subdivided surface, shown in the above figure, 3 times in normal to the surface and then 5 times perpendicular to the surface. Then, while holding the

`Ctrl` key extrude the two connecting faces to complete the handle. **Apply** between extrusions.

8) Make any transformation that you like to make the *Tea Pot* look the way you want.

Section 3: Lid

1) Enter the **Part Design** workbench.

2) Make your **PartBody** the **In Work Object** and then **Insert** a **New Body**.

3) Enter the **Imagine and Shape** workbench.

4) Select the **yz plane** and then select the **Sweep** command. Draw a curve similar to the one shown. Use the **Move Point** option to move the vertices if necessary.

5) Enter the **Part Design** workbench, color your *Tea Pot* how you like and play around with the **Rendering Tools** .

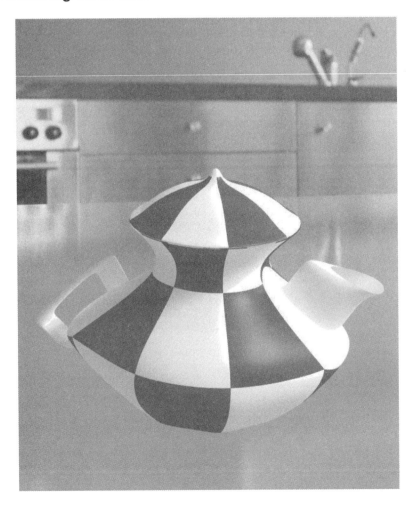

Chapter 7: Exercises

Exercise 7.1: This exercise can be performed after completing the tutorials presented in chapter 7. Model the following parts.

a) An ergonomic computer mouse.
b) A knife
c) A bicycle helmet   .
d) An propeller blade
e) A cell phone

NOTES: